# *Child* WHERE IS MY HONOR?

MICHAEL B. ANNANCY

ISBN 979-8-88685-645-3 (paperback)
ISBN 979-8-88685-646-0 (digital)



Christian Faith Publishing
832 Park Avenue
Meadville, PA 16335
www.christianfaithpublishing.com



Printed in the United States of America

# Contents

# Recommendations

Raising children in today's culture is beyond challenging! Whether it is the easy accessibility of adult material, the time wasting lure of video games, or the intentional indoctrination of today's youth with ungodly values and morals, a book like this can be of the utmost importance. Pastor Michael has taken the time to dig out and unveil timeless biblical truths that will help establish your family on a strong foundation. I encourage you to dive into this book with purpose and intention to allow the Holy Spirit to bring about great change in your life be it one child or one grandchild at a time!!

Pastor Steve Eden
Senior Founding Pastor, Grace Church, Choctaw, Oklahoma
*Author of multiple books, including* Love letters from God, *and* The True You

Michael brings us through three stages of foundational truth and then shows us how to lead, guide, and direct our children. He points out through the word of God that as children grow, they develop from obeying to submission. After laying foundational truths, he finishes up with how to be masters at the game of raising our children. I recommend *Child, Where Is My Honor?*

to all parents whether they are just starting out or desiring to correct their mistakes. Wonderful book with fresh revelation.

David C. Peters
Brownsville, Texas

A powerful message for parents and spiritual parents is laid out in this book by Michael as he shares his heartfelt experiences along with the word of God. As he lays out scripturally and practically how we can and should fight for our children, Michael keeps in front of you the fact that our children's lives are worth fighting for!

Gretchen Cannon
Community Pastor, Grace Church, Oklahoma

This is a story written in a way that gives us all what we need to grow and become what God intended for us to become. I really appreciate how the story ends. Lessons learned at a young age and replicated in other lives today. Proof that truth and instruction in righteousness will never fail to bear fruit. This book both inspired me and challenged me to become a better husband, father, and follower of Christ. In the United States of America, today's families are broken and torn apart. This book mends and heals and gives inspiration and guidance that we all need.

Tom Caton Sr.,
Pastor, Hope Harbor, Choctaw, Oklahoma

*Child, Where Is My Honor?* is a practical biblical approach to effectively handle the perennial challenges of relationships in our time. Special emphasis is placed on the family. Pastor Michael Annancy presents a life application book interestingly written for both parents and children. It is also applicable for those in authority and those under authority. Get one for yourself and for a friend, who will forever be grateful to you for this precious gift. This is a book that will bless you.

Rev. Dr. Abraham Owusu Asare
Senior Pastor, Abundant Gracelife Assembly of
God Church, Oklahoma City, Oklahoma

This is a must read, a great book, a very practical and informative book that will help anyone raise godly children in this generation.

Rev. Edmund Cochrane
Senior Pastor of United Charismatic Healing
Ministry, Edmond Oklahoma

# Acknowledgments

THERE ARE MANY TO WHOM I owe a deep debt of gratitude, beginning with my wife, Mina, who gave me her unwavering encouragement and joy while I was writing this book. But more importantly, she has been my wisest counselor, my most trusted confidant, and a godly wife. Special thanks to my three children: Derrick, Joel, and Michele, who cheered Daddy on while I was completing this work.

I also want to thank my parents, Frederick and Hellen, for teaching us the love of Christ when we were children and taking us to church each Sunday even when we did not get it. You taught us to model our lives after Christ and to put him first above all. For that I am grateful.

I also want to thank my church, Praise Church, for being the great environment where I can communicate God's heart through preaching and teaching his word. Your grace has allowed me to do this work and to share the word of God with other ministries in the United States and abroad.

I also want to thank Pastor Duane and Sue Sheriff of Victory Life Church, whose teachings on family matters have had a major impact on my thinking as a parent and pastor.

Most importantly, I want to thank my Lord and Savior, Jesus Christ, for his grace, and the Holy Spirit's faithful guidance throughout this work.

Michael B. Annancy

# Foreword

## By David R. High

It has been my privilege to know Michael and his family for more than twenty-five years. During that time I have been able to observe his life on many levels. I first met him when he was the director of a Bible school in Ghana. Later when he moved to the United States, he worked for one of my companies for several years, and I was able to observe his character up close. When his family later arrived, my wife, Linda, and I were blessed to get to know them, as well. I can tell you that Michael takes his spiritual life seriously. Now that he is a pastor, I have seen firsthand that his care and responsibility for his flock plays a major role in his life. So when he asked me to take a look at his book, I knew it would be written with the same care and responsibility that I have observed all these years.

You will find that while the title may seem firm or demanding at first glance, Michael does not miss the heart of God on this issue. Our loving heavenly Father wants us to learn respect, not because he wants to keep us in our place, but rather, he knows we were created to thrive under a right understanding of authority. Living grateful and peaceful is a result of giving honor where it is deserved. Michael lays out the case for valuing that outcome.

I pray that the Holy Spirit does for you what only he can do. He is the ultimate truthteller. As you open your heart to his instruction, may he lead you into all truth.

Bless you, Michael, for the love and patience it takes to live it before you write it.

David R. High Senior Pastor,
Grace New Life Church, Oklahoma
Author of *Adopt A Lamb*; *Move Over, Satan: You're in My Seat*; and his most popular to date, *Kings and Priests*

# Introduction

During my work as a therapist with a reputable agency in Oklahoma City, I counseled many troubled four- to eighteen-year-old boys. I made headway with some, but with others, carrying on a conversation was difficult enough let alone suggesting coping skills to help redirect their behaviors positively. While those boys who did work with me gained new insights into dealing with their emotions, those who did not allow me to help continued to exhibit negative behaviors. I was particularly surprised by how they treated their parents even in my presence. They were disrespectful to the highest degree.

Working with troubled kids made me wonder if their rebelliousness, defilement, disrespect, disobedience, and dishonor for their elders were their fault, their parents' fault, or if they were born that way. The disciples asked Jesus a similar question when they came in contact with a man born blind. "His disciples asked him, 'Rabbi, who sinned, this man or his parents, that he was born blind?' And Jesus answered, 'Neither this man nor his parents sinned, but that the works of God should be revealed in him.'" (John 9:2–3).

I compared the way those children behaved to the way my generation was raised and how I behaved growing up. I obeyed and honored my parents (and yes, I still do). In fact, I respect all those who have authority over me. Culturally, I address every lady older than I am with an "auntie" before her first name and every man older than I am with an "uncle" before his first name.

I listened to a tape titled *Raising Wise Children* by Pastor Duane Sheriff. I made an outline of it and used it alongside other materials to teach parents how to instruct, correct, and lead their children in a positive way. These outlines and the word of God make up the basis for this book, which is written from my personal experiences in dealing with kids. It shows why it is important for children to honor their parents and those who rule over them no matter what, even when they pass the age of simply obeying what they say.

Exodus 20:12 says, "Honor your father and your mother, that your days may be long upon the land which the LORD your God is giving you." And Ephesians 6:1–3 says, "Children, obey your parents in the Lord for this is right. 'Honor your father and mother,' which is the first commandment with promise: 'that it may be well with you and you may live long on the earth.'"

This book also makes parents aware of the dangerous world we live in and teaches them that nothing can be taken for granted—our children's lives are worth fighting for. The battle we lose is the one we don't fight.

This book will teach you the importance of raising children according to the word of God to ensure they turn out to be blessings in your life as well as their own.

# *Chapter 1*

# A CHILD IS A BLESSING

Behold, children are a heritage from the LORD,
The fruit of the womb is a reward.
Like arrows in the hand of a warrior,
So are the children of one's youth.
Blessed is the man who fills his quiver with them!

—Psalm 127:3–5

I KNOW WHAT IT IS like to come from a large family. I competed for everything—grades, clothing, shoes, food, and much more. Having "things" is special; not having anything is terrible. My nine siblings and I had almost everything we wanted as children, even though we did not have much. Still, we were content for the most part.

I grew up in a small town and lived in a bungalow. My mom stayed at home while my dad worked as an oven technologist at a glass factory in Ghana, West Africa, making glass soda bottles.

My siblings and I learnt obedience and honor in our early years, and the consequences for disobedience were clearly spelt out. We would have rather been disciplined right away than heard the words, "We will settle this later," or "I will 'beat' [spank] you soon." Most of the spankings were crafted so that no one knew they were coming. Sometimes I could tell when I did something that deserved a spanking, while other times I was not sure if I deserved one.

We were our parents' children who were to please them at all costs without arguing or challenging their authority. We could not ask why, and we needed no explanation. Dad was a great dad in all aspects, but we never wanted to see his anger. He never exhibited it toward our mom, just toward us as his children. It was as if my dad was under pressure to raise perfect children when he was nowhere near perfect himself, and this led to constant spankings, scolding, warnings, and raising of his voice.

Many parents fall prey to this pressure of raising perfect children, something no one can do. If you do not want your children to embarrass or disappoint you, then don't have any because that is what children do. The Bible says that parents are to have godly seeds, not perfect children. Parents are to guide their children in the fear of the Lord, not in the fear of having imperfect children.

My dad was the only educated child in his family. He had a high school diploma and the opportunity to study overseas. His culture demanded that he prove to his siblings and friends he was better than they were and had acquired a great set of skills through education and living abroad to show his children. There is no set manual to parenting; it is on-the-job training, and you can make or break your children if you do not understand the purpose of parenting.

He also had to extend help to many of his siblings' children because he was the youngest and had received financial help and free housing from his older siblings, and he would have done anything to reciprocate what they had done for him.

Long before I knew Ephesians 6:1–3 was in the Bible, my siblings and I obeyed our parents: "Children, obey your parents in the Lord, for this is right. 'Honor your father and mother,' which is the first commandment with promise: 'that it may be well with you and you may live long on the earth.'"

Obedience and honor toward Mom and Dad came naturally, though sometimes with a little hesitation with Dad for fear of what he could do. Mom respected us and worked with us, so we did what we knew to do. When we got out of line, she spanked us, not in excess, but out of love, and explained to us why she did so.

Dad, on the other hand, was unpredictable at times. We could be having a very healthy conversation about school or birthdays together as a family, but then he would snap because someone said something or misunderstood him. We would reconvene later when he thought it was necessary. I call those times the "between moments": between a good family gathering and the snap. These moments damage our hearts and feelings. This made us respond to his questions very carefully. But for the most part, he was very gentle and funny. We honored him more than just out of reverence. We honored him because he was our father and we loved him. We also honored him to escape unnecessary rebukes and so we did not look bad in the presence of our other siblings. However, honoring while mumbling, complaining, and bellyaching while doing what you have been asked to do is not honoring.

My dad started first grade when he was ten years old. He was the biggest, tallest, and roughest, so he was feared by his mates. They actually used him as protection. He fought for them and made sure they were not harassed by the upper graders.

He graduated high school when he was twenty-four years old. He had to learn to fend for himself and make ends meet at that young age. The way he raised his children reflected his upbringing and survival.

My parents did what they knew to do. Both their parents attended church with them, and they continued in it. They were religious. Religion only decorates your outside while leaving your inside ugly. They had their moments and challenges. They went to church as a ritual every Sunday, yet they did not have a personal relationship with Christ. They were very good people and kind to our neighbors and the community. My mom and dad were local preachers and they ministered some Sundays at church. It was later in life when I spoke to them more about Christ that they became born again and accepted Jesus as their personal Savior. When they did not know Christ as their personal Savior, they still trained us in the things of the God, to love one another and be kind to others. My parents were loving and caring—the best things that could ever happen to my siblings and me, but they had their flaws, just as many parents do.

Permit me to share a few of my childhood experiences to drive a point. I am the second of ten children. Nine of us lived with our parents at home and one child lived in Germany. The first three children, of whom I am the middle one, endured some hard training. When, sister K was twelve, I was ten, and brother P was eight, my dad, who was an ex-Boy Scout leader in our little town, woke us up at 5:00 a.m. every day to run two miles and march around the bungalow in routine regiments, singing, chanting, and saluting as if we were soldiers.

My dad would blow a whistle, and in less than five minutes, we had to be out of bed and lined up on the street in front of our bungalow, ready to run and march, with him running and marching behind us. The only way we could get out of our physical training was if something came up or if we were sick. This went on for years until we all went to high school, which was a boarding school and miles away from home.

Not to mention, my first school was a mission school. A mission school is a religious school originally developed and run by Christian missionaries. After our daily marching and running in the mornings, we walked two miles to and from school. All the kids in town walked to their schools and back. There were no school buses then. Just a handful were dropped off by their parents. But it was lots of fun to be walking with other kids from different schools, and at some point, we would branch off and go our different ways to school.

We began our education in a Methodist primary school, and our next-door neighbor's kids attended the Catholic primary school because they attended the Catholic Church. We were Presbyterians, and "Presby" did not have a school of its own.

When I was in the fourth grade, Tarkwa Goldfields Preparatory School opened in another town twelve miles away. It was a much better school compared to the first facility and quality of teachers, so I was transferred there to continue my elementary education. This time, I went by bus. So after my morning march and run each morning, I walked two miles to the bus stop and rode twelve miles on the bus, to and from school.

Our parents loved us. They expressed that love through the things they bought us, the sitting together, and the story times. If we needed a new pair of shoes, we just asked, and we would get it. Every night, we would go into our parents' room and stand around the bed, and Mom would sing a song and say a prayer with us before we went to bed. This was part of the way she taught us obedience and honoring God. If she was not available by the time we went to bed, our elder sister would lead the prayer. There were times our night watchman, a Christian who was responsible for patrolling the bungalows for safety, would call us out of the house after dinner, sit with us on the staircase, and teach us Bible lessons and Christian songs. That is where we learnt most of what we know about God and the Christian life.

We also had a poultry farm, located under our bungalow. One part had hens that laid eggs, another part had the broilers raised for meat, and a third part housed the little chicks. The bungalow was elevated on several pillars and all underneath was space where we had our poultry. We were in the countryside of town and there were bushes all around us. Some days in the middle of the nights, a snake or two would find their way into the poultry farm to either swallow the chicken eggs or to kill the birds. In the middle of the night, when we heard the chickens making unusual noises, we knew an intruder was there, and we had to get up to go kill or remove it.

We had to attack these snakes as a unit, quiet and in a good formation so that we would not kill the chickens instead. Sometimes red ants attacked the chicken, and we had to remove all the chickens and spray the ants out.

We lived mostly on the produce of our farm and bought other things like rice, salt, and oil from the market. We cleared the land, seeded it, and harvested it by ourselves. We also had a piggy pool, and when we slaughtered a pig, our family would keep part of it, and then my brother, P, and I would take what was left to the marketplace, with a weighing scale to sell it ourselves.

These were some of the ways we bonded as a family. My parents never owned a vehicle, so as a family everything was on foot: working on the farm, working at the marketplace with our parents, walking to church, or plucking coconuts in our back-yard and eating them a family. In the evenings, we sat together to pray and share Bible lessons.

We were very present and respectful at home and helped around the house. We served well and were rewarded. My dad taught us a song to sing to attract customers while selling pork. He also taught us to be courteous and polite and to use good manners at all times. He showed us how to relate to people and how to treat our customers with dignity.

We always felt loved and valued, no matter how bad he felt, and no matter how much he spanked or punished us. In many places and cultures, children are often regarded as unplanned, burdens, and inconveniences. Some even despise them or see them as property. These days, some are hardly seen as beautiful additions into hearts and homes.

Children are a gift according to Psalm 127:3. They are a reward from God, not a punishment. A gift is something we do not work for; we simply receive it. That is what God does for us as parents. Parents do not create children; they are merely a channel through which their children come. That is why you cannot choose you children's gender, features, and looks. You contribute to their way of life and growth. You train them, nurture, and instruct them. Because they live with you, and because they came from God, you have all the responsibility to raise them in the discipline and the teaching of the word of God.

When people talk to me about the challenges they face in parenting, especially with teenagers, I tell them, "Well, every child in their teenage years act almost the same." There are no perfect children, and there are no perfect parents. God did not call us to raise perfect children; he called us to raise godly seed. You can't lose focus on that, or you will make them miserable.

Many parents try to live their unfulfilled lives through their children, forcing them to be what they could not even be as Christians. God is calling us to train children to make a difference in their world, not to be perfect.

As parents we have to learn that children mess up and stuff happens. If you spend all your energy trying to make the child perfect, you will fail. Parents need to get their minds off the problems with their children and get their minds on solutions.

Have you as a parent trained, nurtured, invested, disciplined, blessed, and prepared your children to make it in the world, even though they sometimes make poor decisions? Every parent's wish is to see their children and their children's children prosper and live long on this earth. Unfortunately, I have friends who come to my home and say, "Wow, your children are all grown, and soon, they will be out of the house," I wonder what makes them think parenting ends when the children grow up. God never stops being our Father when we reach a certain stage of life or level of maturity.

It is imperative to prepare your children to affect the society they live in positively, not necessarily in big ways, but in little acts of kindness, fulfilling their purpose of being like Christ and reaching others with Christ. You cannot be disengaged in your children's lives and let social media raise them. You cannot give them an Xbox and think they will be okay.

Surprisingly, more than ever, today's children have been left in the hands of daycares, social services, grandparents, and other nonprofit organizations to raise them. This undermines parental authority to its core.

I know a family who is very happy when they drop their children off at daycare. One time they told me, "It relieves our stress and calms us down." What a shame. Daycare is not a place to raise children; it's a place we take our little ones so we can go to work or do something while they are in the care of others. It is not to take a break from parenting. After all, what godly instructions would your children receive from these attendants if they do not have Christ themselves?

Do you even know these attendants and the kind of spirit they operate in? I am not putting down the great work and contribution the daycares or other facilities provide to society, and I know for some people daycare is a must because both spouses work. For others their schedules call for daycare for their children no matter what. I just know it's not the place to rely on to raise children. God has given us, the parents, the mandate to raise them, not the Department of Human Services.

Every single child is a reward and a blessing from God and a source for the growth of his kingdom here on earth, whether they're bringing us pride and happiness; whether they are teaching us how to be more patient, trusting, and forgiving; or whether they are bringing shame and a blot to us. God chooses children to bring us closer to him and help grow our Christian character. They can seem like a curse to us, but that is not what they are intended to be.

I had a distant relative who had seven children. She saw parenting as a wasteful, non-rewarding job. She called herself *Ajumajan*, meaning "useless job." She said she did not find any good in any of her children, so she was going to give birth until one came out good. To her, they were more of a curse than a blessing simply because she refused to learn patience and forgiveness through her children.

This distant relative, like countless others, was disappointed in her children because they did not meet her expectations. See, most parents deceive themselves as to what they want from their children. When a child is quiet, the parents want to take the child to see a doctor; when the child is jumpy, playful, and active all day, they are looking for someone to diagnose them with ADHD.

Sadly, her experience may be bad, yet if she would have focused on the positive things in her children instead of the negative, she would have seen the good in them. After all, many came out good, got married, had families, and had great jobs. There are always lessons in whatever we go through, whether good or bad. And God is able to turn even the bad things into good for us.

Children are no accident regardless of where or how they were conceived. God determined the day of their birth long before they arrived on this earth. As the psalmist wrote, "Your eyes saw my unformed substance; in your book were written, every one of them, the days that were formed for me, when as yet there was none of them" (Psalm 139:16). Children are a gift from God, and their parents should thank God for them. What greater joy is there than to be at the birth or hear the news that a child of yours has been born?

When Jesus taught his disciples about humility, he pointed them to the nature of children. He took a child in his arms "and said, Truly I say you, unless you repent (change, turn about) and become like this little child [trusting, lowly, loving, forgiving], you can never enter the kingdom of heaven [at all]" (Matthew 18:3, AMPC). He was saying that everyone must humble themselves like a child. They must have a childlike faith, and they must trust in the Savior, or they cannot be saved. God will oppose anyone who is proud, but will extend his grace only to the humble (James 4:6).

If this world were full of only infants and toddlers, we would not have most of the social problems we have today. Segregation and racism would perhaps not exist, sin would be at its minimum, wickedness would not be here, and rulership would be enjoyable.

Jesus also said that those who would offend one of these children would be in serious trouble with the Father in heaven because He sees everything that happens to them. Be careful what you do to a child. If you leave a child alone, their faith will move mountains, and that child will live up to their full potential. The moment an adult comes into that child's life, everything changes because we pollute and distort their thinking with what we know. Matthew 18:10 says, "Take heed that you do not despise one of these little ones, for I say to you that in heaven their angels always see the face of My Father who is in heaven."

I am not a grandfather yet, but I understand that grandparents take great joy in their grandchildren, especially when they are little. They love to pick them up, attend school and social functions with them, and "spoil" (bless) them with gifts. Solomon, who probably had grandchildren by the time he wrote Proverbs, wrote that children are like a crown to their grandparents and the glory of their parents (Proverbs 17:6). In other words, they are very proud of them, and they are most precious in their sight.

For grandparents, it's like having their own children all over again, correcting all the things they failed to do or wished they had done better in parenting, only without all the responsibility all over again. God is good, and he gives us second chances so we can mend our ways in every area of life.

As much as children are a blessing from God, parents do have a part to play to get them to the point God is expecting them to get to. Every adult has been a child. So when our children leave home they can reach their target if we as parents have done our job properly. In the next three chapters, I will introduce you to three stages of personalities that confront a child: 1) the simple one, 2) the scorning one, and 3) the foolish one.

# Chapter 2

# THE SIMPLE ONE

**How long, you simple ones, will you love simplicity?**
For scorners delight in their scorning,
And fools hate knowledge.

—Proverbs 1:22 (emphasis mine)

LET ME TELL YOU ABOUT a time I felt simple and naive. In 1999, I traveled out of Accra, Ghana, in West Africa, for the first time, to attend a mission conference in Tulsa, Oklahoma. Lots of things were impeding my normal, everyday life.

Although I spoke English fluently, I still could not fully understand people of non-African descent because they spoke too fast and used too much slang. I also could not figure out how much money I had in my pocket.

My entry point was John F. Kennedy International Airport in New York, enroute to New Jersey to visit my family. After a week in New Jersey, I boarded a Greyhound bus to Tulsa. At the bus station, I asked the driver, "Sir, when are we getting there? Tulsa, Oklahoma, I mean."

"In the morning," he answered.

I had the itinerary correct, but I could not understand what it said.

It was about 2:00 p.m. on a Sunday, and I expected to be at the bus station in Tulsa Monday morning. So, I called my folks and told them when I would arrive.

"What time?"

"Not sure," I responded, "but you can come by at 9:00 a.m. to get me. Or I will find a way to call when I get there."

The journey started, and the bus filled up. We made two stops, and people got off at each station, then got back on as we continued our journey. I personally did not get off because it was not morning yet. Two more stops, and I realized we had a different driver. Around 7:00 a.m., we came to a stop at another station, and we were asked to get off and collect our luggage because we were changing buses and drivers. I was confused. *Did I miss my stop?* I wondered. I got off the bus, but I was anxious, shaking, and confused.

I got my luggage off the bus and walked into the bus station to check in at the front desk to see if I was still on the correct journey to Tulsa or if I had messed up. I showed them my ticket, and to my surprise, I was told I was okay but I would be in Tulsa on Tuesday at 11:00 a.m. What a pity. My ignorance drove me into simplicity.

On the bus, there were guys wearing camouflage Army uniforms and cracking jokes, and people were laughing, but I was not interested in that. I did not understand any of their jokes or their intonation. It seemed as though every word they used was slang and they talked in a weird way not conversant with me. Where I come from, soldiers are to be taken seriously. They can pound on you and mistreat you at a glance. I also could not distinguish the real soldiers from those who were just dressed in camouflage. While I can look back and laugh at this, at the time my thoughts were racing because we kept changing drivers and buses.

Finally, we made it to Tulsa. Thank God I made it. I had been eating cookies and chips for two days and sipping water that I had brought with me. Each time I got off the bus and went into the station to look at the display board to see what they were serving, none of the food sounded familiar, and I was not sure if I could communicate well enough to buy anything.

As simple as I was, at the Tulsa bus station, while I was waiting for my guest to pick me up and take me to the house, I saw both adults and children go to the vending machine to get stuff. It was such an easy thing for them. I went closer to see what was in it, and I found a few things I could possibly eat. Then I was faced with another challenge: I had never used a vending machine. Where was I supposed to insert the cash or the change? How much should I have put in? I was not sure of the exact amount and feared that if I put in more money than required, I was not going to get my change back.

I walked closer and to the side of the machine. Out of the corner of my eye, I tried to see how people were operating it, but I still could not figure it out. So, I gathered enough courage to stand in front of the machine and think about what I should do. Within seconds, a woman came from behind me and stood at my side. Out of nowhere, she said to me, "You don't have to go to school to operate this. Are you a dummy?" and walked away.

If only she had known where I had come from, how long I had been on the bus, how hungry I was, and how naive and simple I was with things around me. She could have helped me. All I needed was grace and a nonjudgmental person—an angel—to help me.

I did not say anything back to her. I merely turned and looked at her as she walked to her seat, still staring at me. I still could not figure out how to use the machine, so I just walked to a seat in the corner to wait on my host, who had been called earlier by a woman who sat next to me on the bus and was interested in my story as a missionary from Africa.

Is this not what many of us as parents do to our children? We judge them by our standards. We match their age with ours and our knowledge about things with theirs. Just because they are our children, we expect them to be proficient in things we have not guided them in. We automatically assume because they go to school and to church and because they socialize with other children, they should have known it. Just because the lady could operate a vending machine, that did not mean any other person could. She lost the opportunity to extend a helping hand, to teach me how to use it, or to just guide me in using it. God would have put that blessing on her account. I would have said,

"Thank you" or just smiled at her in return. Instead, I left as I came. Later that week at a Kenneth Hagin, Sr., camp meeting in Tulsa, I found a vending machine and learnt how to use it.

I have heard over and over the phrase, "Nobody wants to raise a fool," or "Your mama did not raise a fool." Yet we have a society full of fools, and most of the time it is not by accident, just like raising a functional child does not happen by accident. Nobody is born a fool; a fool is self-made.

Scripture simply says the first state we all go through is the *simple one*, naivete. The word *simple* implies extreme vulnerability. It literally means "having no covering, to be opened up or exposed." The simple open their minds to any passing thought and their arms to any passing stranger, regardless of the truth. In other words, the simple lack discernment. A simple person has an oversimplified view of life and fails to recognize the cause-and-effect sequences that affect every area of life, now and in the future.

When I was in the fifth grade, I had a friend who was very, very good at roller skating. Even though he came from a wealthy home, he did not have much more than I did, but he had roller skates, so he was richer than I was by my childlike standard. His mom was from Poland, and his dad was from Ghana. His father met his mom when he worked for the gold mines and was stationed in Poland. I was intrigued when he became my friend.

Fridays after school we went to his house for lunch and then to the clubhouse for Ms. Hoe's swimming class. He would tell me many stories, and I would believe everything he said. I would even tell others all that he told me and brag on him.

I realized from the reactions of other classmates that almost everything he had told me was a lie. For a year, I believed he kept a horse in his house in a room next to his, even though I never saw the horse and I never heard a sound from that room, which was actually his parents' room. He would entice me to try his skates, and he would laugh every time I fell.

I was naïve. I just loved our friendship so much that I believed every lie and trick he played on me. I was simple. I had no facts to cross-check to determine if he was lying to me, so I went along. Thank God he did not do anything bad or unacceptable to me and he did not lead me to do anything stupid or evil. I was not under enormous pressure to buy in to his deceit; I just loved him and followed along. We live in a time of serious peer pressure with everybody trying to blend in and be cool. But being cool is not a ticket to acting foolishly.

Here is the problem. Because the simple are not discerning, they are easily captivated by all kinds of enticements and deceptions. That is how my friend preyed on me. He knew I did not get it, and because he had more than I did, and because I always assumed he was telling me the truth, he could use his influence to manipulate me and entice me with what he had.

Parents have to instruct the simple, teach them, and discipline them, or they will break loose into deception. Oftentimes, the child will run with a gang because he does not have the required leadership at home. And if a child does not have sufficient leadership at home, he will crave leadership and run with a crowd that does drugs, drinks alcohol, buys porn, and does every other bad thing and be persuaded to go along.

Surprisingly, wicked dealers in any trade will tell these children that this is how they will get ahead in life. After all, we are all looking for wealth, so school is not that important. All we need to do in life is make money and live well regardless of whether we are well educated, and this is the best way to make money "fast." This is how to get a fancy car as well as have a classy home, a fat bank account, and a fun and easy life. And kids who crave leadership will buy in no matter how good you think they are. I have seen many children from good, well-disciplined homes turn defiant and out of control because of other kids who preyed on them.

The simple are dangerously immature, extremely gullible, and intensely curious. In the absence of instruction and consistent discipline, the simple will naturally become more and more simple, and our children will not understand anything unless they are taught. The simple are especially vulnerable to seduction because they lack an understanding of the irreversible consequences of moral failure. Morality cannot be legislated; hence, the need to instruct and discipline is vital.

The book of Proverbs provides instruction for the simple. Scorners always seek out the simple and try to become their heroes, mislead them, and mock them. Therefore, protecting the simple ones from the destructive influence of scorning fools means bringing swift correction. It says, "Strike a scoffer, and the simple will become wary" (Proverbs 19:25). Correcting or disciplining one who scorns brings awareness to the simple and helps them understand the dangers.

Certainly, uninformed and uninvolved parents can contribute to raising a simple child. Parents who sit on the sidelines may contribute to their child becoming simple if they continue to neglect their basic parenting skills. I found myself to be simple because of ignorance and cultural limitations. I hear a lot of parents lazily and naively say, "I don't care what my child turns out to be. I am doing my part by providing all the essential amenities of life, and that is all I can offer." But that is just not enough. Things do not shape the lives of our children. It's our mandate to do our part according to the knowledge that God gives us. They need to "be there" to give themselves to their children.

A lot of children spend almost the first half of their lives fighting the authority of their parents, teachers, mentors, police, and even their pastors. They talk about their rights and what pleases them, and argue and wrestle with those in authority over issues and instructions because they hate anyone who points out their mistakes and faults. And when they mature into adults, they spend the other half of their lives fighting their children, because they realize their children are digging the wrong holes and setting traps for themselves. The simple live for the moment and hate to be pointed in the right direction. They have a carefree spirit and lifestyle. They do not think about tomorrow because they hate responsibility and accountability and can't see past today.

When the younger of my two sons was in high school, he loved to argue his way with authorities. He did not like to be stopped and directed to truth. He always said, "It's all about me," meaning it was his choice whether or not to finish school. He did not miss school, but he would not do his assignments and was getting bad grades. He thought he could just slide out of high school and start making money. But while he was working his first job, he realized he needed his education to support his future.

Like the vulture, the simple put off everything they intend to do. The vulture is said never to build its nest. Anytime it rains, it sits in the rain and cries, "Tomorrow I will build my house." Then when tomorrow comes, the vulture still cries, "Tomorrow I will build my house." And it never does.

One thing that ensnares the simple is marketing commercials. The simple love flashy things and do not know that not all that glitters is gold, not all who wear a dress are girls, and not all who wear pants are boys. The simple don't see evil coming. They see only the glittering of a cheap and faulty life. Proverbs 22:3 says, "A prudent man foresees evil and hides himself, But the simple pass on and are punished."

Your children cannot see the dangers ahead of them. There is a reason why parents give birth to children and not the other way around: because parents have experience in the things of life and were here before the children came.

Parents, you are the ones God gave insight and knowledge to so that you can foresee the dangers children will encounter, so you ought to instruct them in the way they should go. Children, follow your parents as they follow the Lord. Paul said, "Imitate me, just as I also imitate Christ" (1 Corinthians 11:1). Truly, the parents are the first examples their sons and daughters emulate. They have to instruct the simple, teach them, and discipline them or they will turn out to be scorners.

Look at what Deuteronomy 6:6–7 says:

> "And these words which I command you today shall be in your heart. You shall teach them diligently to your children, and shall talk of them when you sit in your house, when you walk by the way, when you lie down, and when you rise up."

As parents, you may not be able to have devotions at the dining room table every day with your children. But you should make the effort to teach them while you drive them to school or to their games every day or while you're traveling on family vacations. And when you're home, include the word of God in your everyday conversations.

Every parent has at least some good in their heart to guide their children on a wholesome path of life. Your silence means a lot, and voicing your thoughts is also very important. According to scripture, parents are to teach diligently what is right to their children, whether it is something they learnt from intuition or from experience. It's a process that thrives, not ends. If the children stop learning, they stop growing.

# Chapter 3

# THE SCORNING ONE

How long, you simple ones, will you love simplicity?
**For scorners delight in their scorning,**
And fools hate knowledge.

—Proverbs 1:22 (emphasis mine)

IT IS SAID THAT PRACTICE makes perfect. It is also true that what you focus on will have your attention. If the simple ones are not informed and taught, if they are not disciplined, if they are not corrected, and if they are not stopped, they have the potential to become scorners.

Surprisingly, many scorners are parents because they were never disciplined out of their simplicity. Any person can be a scorner. You can be rich and still be a scorner. You can be in the highest seat of the land and still be a scorner. You can be educated from the best school and still be a scorner. You can be a CEO and still be a scorner. You can have nothing and still be a scorner. I know a few of them.

The word *scorner* means "to purposefully say things without authoring them." It means "to mimic and mock people while denying the facts." Scorners are great at calling people names only to belittle them in order to have power over them or to cast doubt at their character and make them feel insignificant.

Scorners dominate the simple and bully others. They seek followers and coerce them with foolishness. They use the simple to fulfill their agendas and reward them with little or nothing at all. If you are not loyal to a scorner, he will make it known that you don't exist and will say that those who rise in opposition are weak or have a low IQ or no energy.

The scorner's facial expressions communicate the disdain and contempt that he has in his heart toward authorities. These include parents, civil authorities, and God. Scorners break the law and laugh at it. They find every opportunity to make others look weak. They say what they cannot do and hate competition.

When I was in junior high, there was one particular boy in our class—Silas N.—who was a scorner. In those days, soccer was part of our P.E. class, but he never showed any interest in being part of the team. He just showed up on the field because it was a requirement. But he never contributed anything positive to his team, nor did he promote growth and stability. Silas had no praise or cheers for his team. He was there only to laugh at the way the other pupils played soccer. By the end of each practice, he always had a funny name for almost every kid on the field, and he would make fun of everything that happened that day.

He was quick to judge anyone who made a wrong move, and he was loud and insensitive to others. He always referred to himself as the smartest and the coolest, but he was annoying and worrisome. Anytime he was caught doing something he should not do, he was quick to blame other people for his mistakes.

Scorners like Silas think they know it all. In class, he tried to answer every question the teacher asked. Even when it was not his turn to answer, he would whisper something just to get the attention of the other kids. Most of the time, his answers were wrong, but he would insist the teacher did not hear what he said, or the teacher's answer was wrong. He loved to study big words out of the dictionary to impress people. We called him "the King of Tautology." He was always unaware when he used the same phrase twice in one sentence.

Silas claims to have been everywhere in the world, seen everything in the world, and tasted every food in the world. If you tried to argue with him, he made it seem as though you were jealous of his achievements. Nobody wanted him as a friend, nor did he care to be a friend to anyone who would not bow to his foolishness.

If you told him to stop calling you names, he would just call you more names. The only way out was to avoid him or not be bothered when he called you a name. Anyone who got angry at the name-calling fueled his ego and foolishness.

A scorner not only rejects truth; he denies truth. Tell a scorner it is dangerous to walk on broken glass and he will try and walk on it. Then, when the scorner cuts himself on the glass, he will deny it and attempt to walk on the broken glass again to prove he is not weak.

The scorner has also embraced that which is abominable to God. Psalm 1:1 describes the progression of foolishness and sin, referring to a man who first walks "in the counsel of the ungodly," then stands "in the way of sinners," and finally sits "in the seat of the scornful." Like Silas, the scorner utterly detests people and ideas that contradict his false thinking, and he expresses the scorn through derisive attitudes, behavior, and speech.

Here are some scriptures I want you to get abreast of, which the scorner turns a deaf ear to and rebukes. Proverbs 13:1 says, "A wise son heeds his father's instruction, But a scoffer does not listen to rebuke." Those who attempt to lead the scorner away from the path of destruction that he seems determined to follow will suffer his wrath. Proverbs 15:12 says, "A scoffer does not love one who corrects him, Nor will he go to the wise." Scorners hate morality and righteousness. They are blind to truth and doing what is right or good. Proverbs 9:7–8 says:

> He who corrects a scoffer gets shame for himself,
> And he who rebukes a wicked man only harms himself.
> Do not correct a scoffer, lest he hate you;
> Rebuke a wise man, and he will love you.

Again, a scorner must be disciplined for his own sake and for the sake of those he can potentially influence. I am not talking about abuse; I am talking about correction. Most children of scorners become scorners themselves because that is all that they have known and they have not received any alternative discipline to guide and curb their behavior. Most children of scorners fall into the trap of scoring because they want their parents' affirmation.

I see the way fathers scorn their children, but the children will defend them and call it their right. If you are a scorner, your child will grow up to become a scorner if you don't change. A duck gives birth to another duck. If you quack, he will quack. If you swim, he will swim. If you eat dirt, he will eat dirt. Parents have to get involved in their kids' lives to redirect them. They have to get in the mud and get dirty doing what is right for them.

I recall a story my dad told me about a man who had two beautiful sons. They were well-educated, he gave them everything they needed, and both were successful. One emulated his father, who was a habitual drunkard. He drank himself to bed almost every night. His favorite saying was "Like father, like son. I am my father's image." The other despised drinking because of the shame it brought on his family. Most nights, strangers would carry his father from the side of the road into the house. Children must choose not to repeat the mistakes and weaknesses of their parents.

Scorners, in general, delight in scorning. They admire the life of scorning, and that is how they get their kicks. They are the children who always sit in the back of the class, and when everyone is busy studying, they make paper planes and throw them at people or sneeze loudly and laugh so hard that everyone turns to look at them. They will not pay attention and will not allow others to listen or learn. They boast in their stupidity and assume they know it all. They normalize every one of their stupidities to gain followers, and those who join in laughing and misbehaving lose their sense of morality.

You want to know what a hypocrite looks like? Watch a scorner—they say one thing and do another. They can swear by their words one minute and find a way to back out of them the next. Scorners downplay the seriousness of a matter only to show strength. They hate to be held responsible for their actions. They are double-minded people and dangerous.

Watch how they blame things on other people: "But the people said" or "Well, I am okay with it, but the people are not okay with it." In 1 Samuel 15:15, Saul said, "They have brought them from the Amalekites; for the people spared the best of the sheep and the oxen, to sacrifice to the LORD your God; and the rest we have utterly destroyed." Saul was the one given the instruction to destroy everything and everyone, but he spared them and then blamed his actions on the people. This is typical of a scorner. They never apologize because they believe it is a sign of weakness. They dig even bigger holes for themselves by making false assertions even before an event happens to justify their failure or defeat. Failure is not a good teacher to the scorner; it means weakness.

In church, the scorner is usually the kid who sits in the back and has no respect for the pastor when he is speaking. Instead of listening to the pastor's message, the scorner is usually watching a movie or a clip. He is in church, but his heart is somewhere else. He is busy engaging with others at a distance.

He doesn't care to be part of the service, but he laughs when others laugh as if he is. He is quick to say, "I have heard this sermon before," "I have had this class before," and "I know it all." If there are twenty kids in class, and the scorner ends up placing eighteenth or nineteenth on the list after a test, he is bold to tell you to your face, "If you turn the list upside down, I come in second or third."

He likes to mock people and is very disruptive. He puts others down, and if everything is not about him, then no one gets any praise or the last laugh. Scorners know all; you know nothing. In Ghana, they are called *Konongo kaya*, the one who will neither carry the load nor allow others to carry it. If he sees you approaching the load, he acts as if he is going to carry it, but the moment you leave, he drops it. They act like crabs in a pot; they are not ready to climb out, but when anyone else tries to do it, they pull that person back into the pot. They will do anything and everything to get you to the bottom.

Scorners never give people credit. They will discredit your achievements, making them seem fraudulent and undeserving. Scorners take the credit for everything that is profitable and that everyone can see. They argue their way out of everything and every situation to look and sound good in the eyes of others. They are full of discontent for all authority. They easily call people names to discredit them and have no respect for the elderly.

Scorners cannot reward good behavior. They are not good at obeying instruction. They always wants to outsmart others with their bad behavior and have no respect for their parents. If these behaviors are not stopped, the scorner will spiral downward and become a fool.

There is hope for the simple, and there is some hope for the scorner if his behavior is corrected quickly, but there is little hope for anyone who turns into a fool. So stop your child from descending into a fool.

If you are the parent and you have allowed the scorner to progress as far as he has without correction and instruction, you have done a lot of damage. I have known many fathers who believe in "Each one for himself, and God for us all." They are disengaged in their children's discipline. They tell their children, "I brought you into the world, and it is your duty to become what you want to be." These parents make little effort to shape the lives of their children.

If your child degenerates into a scorner, you can't correct him anymore, and you can't tell him anything. Your child thinks he knows everything. He will not receive your correction or rebuke, and that is dangerous.

The scorners are not here to say, "Please show me something," "Teach me something," or "Correct me if I am wrong." They hate you in their hearts and despise you if you try to correct them. Correction, like repentance, means to turn around completely or make a drastic shift away from danger. You can show them much love and grace, but they won't budge.

Scorners like their ways. They like their lives, and you coming in to correct them depicts them as weak and they think you've come to take their authority away. They love power, and they never apologize because they're afraid of losing ground. They say one thing and then either deny it the next or change what they said to mean something else.

They live in the present. Their past does not matter to them. It is good to disregard your past and process your present only if you have learnt the lessons from the past and are not going to repeat them. Scorners have a selective memory. They choose what they will remember, and everything else is not their problem, even if it continues to tie them to the wrong things.

Scorners live as though they are mysterious superheroes on assignment to protect something special for themselves because everyone who came before them is a failure and cannot accomplish what they can accomplish. They are here to make a name for themselves and to save everybody because no one is competent enough to save themselves.

They wake up forgetting what happened yesterday; all their effort is focused on solving today's problems their way. They need no imputes from anyone. Your position is a deterrent to their success. Everyone else's ideas are fishy to them, and if they fail in something they purposed to do, then it was the people who failed them. They live in a world deprived of reality.

Correcting them leaves you, the helper, a surprise beyond measure. Sometimes their response may cause you never to get involved when you have a solution for them. See, you cannot tell young people anything. You cannot help them, you cannot reach out to them, and you cannot correct them. They would hate you for the good in you. It is difficult for a child who has become a scornful person to be corrected. You cannot preach to that child; it will fall on deaf ears, on hard ground.

Trying to teach a scorner is like pouring water on a rock— it goes nowhere, it will not yield anything, and sometimes you will have to discipline him to help him find alternative coping skills that promote positive thinking.

I repeatedly emphasized to one of the young guys I was counseling that he would be shot dead or end up in prison before too long. He was fifteen and constantly getting himself into trouble. He had already been kicked out of three junior high schools and one other school that helped kids with behavior problems finish high school. He had also been held in a juvenile detention center for stealing and crushing a stolen vehicle, which he blamed on his friends and on his mother's boyfriend, who lived at home with them.

He told me he liked to skip school to punish his mom. He was sleeping on the living room couch because the house he lived in had three rooms: his mother and her boyfriend were sharing one; his older sister, her boyfriend, and a newborn were sharing another; and his two other sisters were sharing the last room. He needed a room to himself. He blamed his truancy on a lack of space at home and not having any privacy. He began staying out with friends and eventually got caught up in a gang.

I have seen the TV show *Beyond Scared Straight*, where they take troubled teens to interact with hardened inmates who try to intervene. Scorners should be introduced to such programs to show them where their destiny lies if they don't mend their ways.

You can take them to the hospital ER and let them see the front-liners rush people in on stretchers, trying to save them. Let them observe how broken people can be when they go out partying and lose control of their lives.

Take them to the insane asylum and let them see people hooked on drugs. Take them under the bridge to show them what homelessness looks like, where they sleep, and how vulnerable they can be to attacks. Teach them to appreciate the opportunities they have and how they can lose them with the lifestyle they are pursuing.

Children who are scorners because they hate correction and direction can give their parents dirty looks when they try to correct them. Even though their looks can "kill," they will go blind because they do not see the danger coming.

The eye that mocks his father,
And scorns obedience to his mother,
The ravens of the valley will pick it out,
And the young eagles will eat it. (Proverbs 30:17)

When I was about twelve years old, we had a neighbor who was a girlfriend of the plant manager who lived next to our bungalow. We lived at number 10 and they lived at number 8, about 120 meters away. The man and his wife had some marital challenges, and they separated. This woman in question is his girlfriend from a small town.

Each time my mom met the man, she would ask, "When are you bringing your wife home and letting your girlfriend go?" The wife and my mom had become friends over the years as the husbands worked at the same glass molding factory. Apparently, this girlfriend did not like that, so she constantly rained insults and said some bad things to my mom.

One day, a friend of my mom witnessed the insults this lady was hurling at her, and the friend said to us children, "When she speaks evil to your mom, go to her and say to her, 'I see why everyone is saying things about you,' and leave it at that."

One day she verbally attacked my mom at our house.

Then my younger sister said what we had been told to say, "I see why everyone is saying things about you."

She became angry and asked, "What are people saying about me?"

We had nothing to say because we did not know anything anyone had said about her. We were only asked to confront her with that statement. As a matter of fact, no one was saying anything about her, but she became worried and never spoke about my mom again. She also eventually left the man.

That is what scorners do. They get others involved in saying things that are not true. We are seeing an increase of scorners in our world as established wisdom is now being rejected in favor of emotion and human opinion.

The scorner lies in wait for every opportunity to pounce on the innocent and the weak to make them seem strong.

# Chapter 4

# THE FOOLISH ONE

How long, you simple ones, will you love simplicity?
For scorners delight in their scorning,
**and fools hate knowledge.**

—Proverbs 1:22 (emphasis mine)

THE MOST DANGEROUS TYPE OF fool is a *steadfast fool*. The word *fool* means "stupid, wicked." It can also be translated as "a vile person"—someone nasty, unpleasant, and horrible. He is like the bile in the chicken, which is very bitter, and if not removed before cooking, it can easily spread through the parts of the chicken when broken (actions), discoloring and destroying the taste and beauty of the chicken. The fool can discolor and make the lives of the people he associates with bitter if not cleaned, disciplined, tamed, controlled, or removed from the lives of the people he is ruining.

The fool has said in his heart,
"There is no God."
They are corrupt,
They have done abominable works,
There is none who does good. (Psalm
14:1)

The fool relies on self to justify his life. He is self-confident and close-minded. I call fools "shallow grave diggers." There is a reason the grave is always dug six feet deep. It's to avoid infections, stop the spread of diseases and smell, and to deter grave looters.

Fools are shallow in their thinking. They are often their own god, freely living in instant gratification, and living an I-don't-care life. Everything goes no matter what people say or think.

A friend told me this story. It was the day he felt foolish. He said that he and his uncle were at a family gathering and his uncle asked him to go somewhere with him before the meals were ready. He was new in town and did not know where he was. He obliged and went. He said he was taken to a small kiosk where they sold locally distilled liquor, "moonshine." They were served some and they drank. Sitting among the family members, he felt something was wrong with him.

He had a feeling his nose and eyes had slightly shifted, so he started twitching his face to try to fix it. He observed that family members were looking at him and wondering why he was doing that. He was so worried they were looking at him that he did it all the more. Finally he was removed to a room where he slept for hours after he learnt he had drunk cannabis-infused alcohol. He had made such a fool of himself.

The fool aims, first of all, to draw as many as possible into his evil ways. He is the yes man and the clown in the family. The fool relies on his emotions as the source of truth and hates knowledge, even though common sense is far more reliable than emotions. He "follows the direction of his stomach." Attempts to reprove him will be futile and bring frustration to the one who tries to do so. Only God can successfully reprove a steadfast fool.

> The fear of the LORD is the beginning of knowledge,
> But fools despise wisdom and instruction.
> (Proverbs 1:7)

Fools despise wisdom and instruction. The scorner despises parents and those in authority. The fool despises the truth; he hates the word of God. The fool sees sin coming at him but does nothing to avoid it or eliminate it. Instead, he embraces sin to see what it is like. Sin is not good; it will take your soul to hell. Sin can bind you, blind you, and grind you like it did to Samson. All sin is pleasurable for a moment. That is why we take the bait from the devil. Fools put down morality and exalt immorality. They ridicule righteousness and exalt unrighteousness.

Proverbs 17:10 says, "Rebuke is more effective for a wise man, than a hundred blows on a fool." So true. Beat a fool, and he will not change. Punish a fool, and he will not change. Lock the fool in prison, and he will come out worse than before. He does not see correction nor change, only rebellion against the law, and refuses to allow anyone turn him on the right path. He sees revenge and hatred as an opportunity to get his way, and when he does not get his way, he goes on a rampage. The fool cannot celebrate people and their achievements. He is quick to forget the good and does not accept constructive criticism.

When you have a fool as your boss, he is open to firing you just for the fun of it. He is always looking for an opportunity to feel fulfilled in doing what is wrong and immoral but right in his head. A fool is threatened by disloyalty and will bring you down, deny knowing you, and speak of everything you did as if you needed his help. A foolish person does not acquire new information. His source of information is hearsay. He is quick to act on what he hears without verifying whether it is true.

A childhood friend of mine married a few years before I did. Anytime he and his wife had a misunderstanding, the wife would smash their China on the ground. Once things went back to normal, she would go to the store and buy a set to replace the set she broke. This happened often. That is typical of a foolish person. They do things to satisfy their whims to the detriments of others. Fools have their own company of friends, yet they exploit others. Paul wrote in 1 Corinthians 15:33, "Do not be deceived: 'Evil company corrupts good habits.'" You become like those you hang out with. You influence them, or they influence you for good or bad. So the one who walks with the wise tends to become wise, but the fool who runs with the foolish will become like them.

If a person runs with people who say there is no God, and God declares such people fools, then he will also start to believe there is no God and become a fool, as well. Only a fool will despise his father's or his mother's instruction because they have more experience, more wisdom, and more common sense. So anyone who despises parental wisdom only shows his foolishness. On the other hand, the person who listens to (heeds) reproof (or correction) is prudent and is no fool at all.

The Christian life is striving to emulate those following after Christ. God has not called parents to raise scorners to become fools. He has called us to raise our children to become wise.

# Chapter 5

# POINT YOUR CHILDREN
# TO THEIR TARGET

Behold, children are a heritage from the LORD,
The fruit of the womb is a reward.
Like arrows in the hand of a warrior,
So are the children of one's youth.
Happy is the man who has his quiver full of them;
They shall not be ashamed,
But shall speak with their enemies in the gate.

Psalm 127:3–5

THIS PASSAGE BEGINS AS AN instruction from David to Solomon as to how to raise children and keep a home. The Lord wants us to continue from generation to generation in a lifestyle of righteousness. Psalm 127:1 says, "unless the LORD builds the house, They labor in vain who build it; Unless the LORD guards the city, The watchman stays awake in vain." Whether you're a single parent, a grandparent, a stepparent, or whether both of you as parents live in the home, you cannot ignore your God-given assignment, or your child will fail in life. Children are the Lord's heritage; they are not ours. Raising our children is not about our name living on. It is about the Lord's name living on through our children from generation to generation as they live in his righteousness. That can happen only if our children know the Lord.

Our country needs us to raise wise children. Matthew 5:16 says, "Let your light so shine before men, that they may see your good works and glorify your Father in heaven." The world needs to see our testimony more than they need to hear it. They need to see us live for Jesus, not just occasionally talk about him.

In today's world, many people are trying to find their ancestors. That is a good and acceptable thing, but it's not that important. I have known people who have traced their heritage only to find out their ancestors were people they did not want to be associated with. What is important is to find your spiritual ancestors.

In Hebrews 11, we find most of our spiritual ancestors who, through faith, changed the world. We have ancestors in our family tree who shut the mouths of lions, worked miracles, parted the Red Sea, and walked on dry ground. They saw horses and chariots swallowed up by water as well as a pillar of cloud by day and a pillar of fire by night. They saw manna fall for forty years and quail for forty years, enough to feed them until they entered the land of abundance, the Promised Land.

To do this parenting thing well, you have to have God in your corner. It is not strength or book knowledge you need to raise children; it is grace. I am convinced that grace is only found in Jesus, and that it allows you to look beyond your limitations and is given as an antidote to failure. It also allows you to embrace the opportunity to stand and fulfill your place as a parent. Even if it does not work well for you, you still did your part and you should not stress. Just relax in the grace that has been with you.

Paul said in 2 Timothy 2:1, "Be strong in grace that is in Christ Jesus" to encourage him to do the work that was ahead of him. Parents need to be strong in grace if their parenting is to go well. Grace is the power of God at work in you to fulfill what he has designed. It's called *divine enablement*. Faith changes things. It overcomes problems. Grace changes people. It keeps problems from overcoming you. Grace is the inner substance that will sustain you as you apply the principles of faith to change things.

So the first thing to realize and understand in order to raise functional children—wise children—is that we need the Lord. He is the source of our strength, our wisdom, and our understanding as parents. If we were perfect parents and we had the perfect parenting manual, we would not be where we are with parenting.

The world has a way of doing things that makes natural sense. God's people have a way of doing things, and God wants us to be guided by his word. So we need to receive instruction from the Lord to raise our children. Our friends, our parents, and our books may be good, but they are not the source. The source is the Lord. There are always two ways of doing things:

the way the world teaches us to do things, and the way the word of God teaches us to do things. We always have to choose.

Psalm 127:4 says, "As arrows are in the hand of a mighty man, so are children of the youth." This verse tells us the importance of children born to young parents with young bodies. "Young" doesn't mean "immature," but from an acceptable age to knowledgeable and mature parents, an age where they have the ability to do things with their children. I have known men in their fifties who have had children and cannot do homework with them, go to their games, play video games, or other things children want to do with their fathers.

Many parents have set childbearing aside to pursue careers, wealth, and possessions. Children are not just some aspiration or possession we have in the Lord. They are called by God to carry on the name of the Lord, to pass his legacy on to future generations. I have nothing against possessions, wealth, and careers, but children are the Lord's heritage to carry his name to the next generation. If you are putting careers and possessions above having children, then you are putting yourself above the heritage of the Lord. Proverbs 17:6 says, "Children's children are the crown of old men, And the glory of children is their father." This means children are a crown to their grandfathers and a glory to their fathers.

Parents and guardians, it is our duty to empty our arrows out of the quiver and point our children in the right direction, so when they are shot out like arrows, they can hit their target through discipline. Like arrows, they have to be formed, shaped, sharpened, and tried over and over. Next they have to be pointed in a direction and released, and we rejoice because they hit their target.

One of the greatest things is not only seeing your children accept Jesus, but also seeing them filled with the Holy Spirit and your grandchildren filled with the Holy Spirit so that they will become disciples who, in turn, disciple others. Acts 2:39 says, "For the promise is to you and to your children, and to all who are afar off, as many as the Lord our God will call."

As parents, we need to disciple our children, and not just let them be followers Jesus Christ. Judas was a follower but he was not a doer of the word. A disciple is one who learns the word and does it. So when the word says "make disciples," God not only wants us to be disciples, but he also wants us to make disciples.

How do we make disciples? Not just by befriending them, taking them to a Christian concert, or inviting them to lunch, but by helping them get into the word of God and observe all things that Jesus commanded. That is what we as parents need to do with our children: disciple them.

My mom lived long enough to see all nine of her children born again and filled with the Holy Spirit and her grandchildren born again and filled with the Holy Spirit. Myself and three of my siblings pastor churches. All of this happened because she continued to teach us the things of God and to help us walk in them by following her example.

My wife and her four siblings are also born again and filled with the Holy Spirit. All three girls are married to pastors, and the two boys are active in church, just as their children will be one day. While our family names carry on, it is more important for us to carry the name of the Lord from generation to generation.

As moms and dads or as single parents, we have to do the shaping and the forming because one day we will have to let our children go. We cannot hold onto them their entire lives. I remember a wealthy family that had two daughters and a son. The father was so strict that he would not allow his children to leave the house after 9:00 p.m. At ages twenty-four and twenty-two, the girls would use a ladder to climb out of the back of the house and return before dawn to avoid getting caught.

Raising children is challenging, but you cannot keep them past a certain age. They need to go their way and explore the world for themselves. They may wobble a bit, they may stray a bit, they may falter a bit, and they may fail and bring you shame, but once you point them in the right direction, they may hit the target of holiness and godliness, and you will rejoice.

No parenting style fits all children, or our children would be perfect. Every parent, through loving them, spending time with them, and nurturing them can get their children to live the best lives they can. It is all up to the parent to adopt what works for that particular child. Like fools, wise children are not born; they are made. That encourages me to know that there is a chance I can bring a child where God wants that child to be.

As parents, God wants to make us mighty warriors because our children are arrows in our hands. But even if you don't have children or they are all grown and out of the house, all of us still have God, our heavenly Father, as our Father.

The person God the Father is to you is the person he wants you to be to your children. What God will not do to you, he will not want you to do to your children. Children have faith, and children believe. You have to teach a child to believe in God and to appreciate other children rather than disliking them.

God gave every one of us as his children the capacity and ability to believe we can become anything we want to be and have everything we want. Parents should be careful, however, not to create a stumbling block for them. We are not to teach our children idol worship and pervert their minds but protect and preserve their innocence against wrong, abuse, and impurity.

If you want to understand how God's kingdom works, you have to understand the heart and faith of the child. Matthew 18:3 says, "Unless you are converted and become as little children, you will by no means enter the kingdom of heaven." To enter into eternal life, you have to become a child. Heed the warning in Hebrews 12:5–9:

> And you have forgotten the exhortation which speaks to you as to sons:
>
> "My son, do not despise the chastening of the LORD,
> Nor be discouraged when you are rebuked by Him;
> For whom the LORD loves He chastens,
> And scourges every son whom He receives."
>
> If you endure chastening, God deals with you as with sons; for what son is there whom a father does not chasten? But if you are without chastening, of which all have

become partakers, then you are illegitimate and not sons. Furthermore, we have had human fathers who corrected us, and we paid them respect. Shall we not much more readily be in subjection to the Father of spirits and live?

# Chapter 6

# LEARNING OBEDIENCE

Children, obey your parents in the Lord, for this is right.

—Ephesians 6:1

SCRIPTURE PROMISES THAT THOSE WHO obey their parents will live long on the earth. If you don't, your time on earth will be short. This can be both spiritual and physical. You can be a dead person inside, living on earth in disobedience. Even though you are alive, because of disobedience, you live as though you're in hell.

Many people are alive but not living a blessed life, and this can be linked with disobedience. Being good, however, does not guarantee a blessed life. You need to have a relationship with the source of those blessings.

I have known many good and kind people who do not have a relationship with their parents and therefore cannot hear and follow their voice. It is the same with God. If you have no relationship with him, you cannot hear or follow him. As children, we, on the other hand, have the ability to follow our parents and obey their voice, which is their authority.

You may not agree with that authority, but you are to submit to it. Submission to authority should bring freedom, not bondage, just as submission to Jesus brings freedom.

Romans 1 helps us understand that all authority comes from God, but that does not mean every parent handles their authority the way God would want. However, the position they stand in is from God. This is not by evolution or choice; it is ordained to be so.

Submission is not obedience, and obedience is not submission. Submission is a heart attitude, and obedience is an outward act. As children, we are to be in submission to our parents because we are under their authority. We are to act in obedience to them, but when their authority violates the word of God and we have to make a choice, we have to gladly and always obey God over man. Anytime something is asked of you and it violates your conscience, you have to obey God.

If a father asks a son to go with him to rob a bank, that son should not conform to his father's wishes. Submission does not mean obeying everything someone asks you to do. Stand for the word of God with a loving, submissive attitude. You should say "no" in submission but not be in obedience to the voice of bank robbery.

Children are told to obey, not submit, because submission requires knowledge, and children are not old enough to have the knowledge to submit, so they are told to obey, for this is right.

As a child growing up, I had a submissive attitude toward my parents, and I did everything I could to obey them. If they told me not to go swimming, I would not go. Often I would have to do something for them and then go swimming later.

You can have a submissive attitude and not be obedient. Bondage is obedience without submission. As a parent, I would rather my children be submissive to me than be obedient without submitting. To make a child to do what you want them to do may cause them to have a rebellious attitude. When children are in submission to their parents, they honor God.

Deuteronomy 4:5–6 says:

> Look, I now teach you these decrees and regulations just as the Lord my God commanded me, so that you may obey them in the land you are about to enter and occupy. Obey them completely, and you will display your wisdom and intelligence among the surrounding nations.

Our children need to be taught how to give obedience out of gratitude. Parents should not demand obedience from their children; it should be freely given to them. Obedience should be given, not demanded. Obedience is not legalism; obedience is not law; and parents, you should not be constantly demanding obedience from your children.

They have to be taught to know to do it. Because you have done so much for your children, their heart's desire should be to give you obedience. How many of us know God is much more pleased when we give to him out of our will rather than out of law. I would much rather have my kids be obedient to me because they want to, rather than laying down a law, slapping them every time, or spanking them every time they disobeyed.

I do not want them to be obedient because they are always fearing I may spank them. I want them to come to a point where they desire to be obedient to me. And that is again what the word of God is saying: "Children, obey your parents in the Lord, for this is right" (Ephesians 6:1).

Obeying your earthly father is obeying God since both represent God's authority here on earth. So if we are going to obey our earthly fathers and live a long life on earth, how much more if we obey our heavenly Father? Doing your Father's will means you will not only live a long life, but you will also abound in every good work.

In addition, 2 John 3:2 says that God wants you, who obey and honor your earthly father, to walk in prosperity and in good health. Beloved, I pray that you may prosper in all things and be healthy, just as your soul prospers.

God's highest desire and every parent's highest desire for their children is that their souls prosper, and right behind it is wealth and health. God is saying, If you follow after me, you would be "blessed shall you be in the city, and blessed shall you be in the country" (Deuteronomy 28:3). He also says, "I will put none of the diseases on you which I have brought on the Egyptians. For I am the LORD who heals you" (Exodus 15:26).

God is saying to his children, If you follow after me, my greatest desire is that "you may prosper in all things and be in health, just as your soul prospers" (3 John 1:2). God is not going to do things your way; you have to follow his way.

Maybe you are waiting for your parents to do something right or change their minds about something you don't agree with. Maybe they wronged you, and you are looking for a resolution to obey them. But Ephesians 6:1 says, "Children, obey your parents in the Lord, for this is right."

One of the principles of God, which is in Luke 6:38, says, "Give, and it will be given to you: good measure, pressed down, shaken together, and running over will be put into your bosom. For with the same measure that you use, it will be measured back to you."

Do you want to live long on earth and prosper so you can own boats, houses, and fat bank accounts? No. God wants you to live a long life in divine prosperity and in divine health so you can spread the gospel.

Job 5:17–18 says, "Behold, happy is the man whom God corrects; Therefore do not despise the chastening of the Almighty. For He bruises, but He binds up; He wounds, but His hands make whole." Again, the bruises and wounds mentioned in this scripture are not physical sickness, pain, and sores. They refer to the chastening with the word of God. Our earthly fathers discipline the flesh, but our heavenly Father uses the word of God to discipline us through our spirits.

2 Timothy 3:16–17 says, "All Scripture is given by inspiration of God, and is profitable for doctrine, for reproof, for correction, for instruction in righteousness." Oftentimes, fools despise discipline, which leads them to destruction. But because discipline is for our own good, God wants us to be happy when he chastens us with his word.

Proverbs 13:24 says, "He who spares his rod hates his son, But he who loves him disciplines him promptly." If you do not discipline your child, you will create anger in that child by not preparing them or disciplining them for the consequences of life. Spanking is someway acceptable, but other things should happen before the paddle is pulled out, the most important of which is speaking and giving the discipline, setting boundaries so the child understands. Neglecting discipline is an act of hate toward your child. Raising children without boundaries is dangerous because this generation is not ready to be responsible to take on the challenge of being a godly seed.

Ephesians 6:1–3 says, "Children, obey your parents in the Lord, for this is right. 'Honor your father and mother,' which is the first commandment with promise: 'that it may be well with you and you may live long on the earth.'"

We have all been children before, and some are still children and will continue to be the children of somebody. Truly, the fact that we were born of women makes us children.

You'll also notice that God adds no conditions to Ephesians 6:1. Without exception, without debate, and without an argument, it says to obey, for this is right. If this is the right thing to do, then it is wrong not to do it.

Your children and my children are under the commandment to obey us as parents. They are to comply with direction unless it violates their conscience or goes against the teachings in the Bible.

When I was born again, I was living with my dad. I had a conversation with him about buying him beer. He was not a serious drinker or a heavy drinker. He drank occasionally with friends, mostly on weekends, and I was the one sent to buy the beer. But I was no longer comfortable buying it because I did not want people to see me go into the liquor shop, and I did not like the fact that I was the one providing the liquor.

There was nothing really wrong with it, but it bothered me so much that I told him I would no longer be buying the liquor for them. It violated my conscience, and that was it. I was glad he understood, and we were happy together.

You as a parent need to instruct your children in the word of God and realize they are to obey you, and this is right. Parents, according to this verse, are the highest authority in a child's life. No one is to undermine parental authority.

The government cannot and should not undermine parental authority. The school system cannot and should not undermine parental authority. The church cannot and should not undermine parental authority. Children are under a commandment to obey you, the parent, for this is right. All these other authorities in the child's life are to support and not take over the parents' authority.

Obedience is the children's conduct; it is their outward action. Children have to be taught what is right and what is wrong, and they have to be taught to obey, to act right, and to conduct themselves according to the ways of God and the word of God.

# Chapter 7

# LEARNING HONOR

"Honor your father and mother," which is the first
commandment with promise: "that it may be well
with you and you may live long on the earth."

—Ephesians 6:2–3

To *HONOR* IS DIFFERENT THAN to *obey*. While obeying deals with
the outer actions, honoring deals with the heart. *Honor* means
"to reverence and respect" your mother and father. *Honor* is "to
esteem highly." Children may not know everything about their
mom and dad, but they honor them because of the position
they stand in.

Parents make mistakes, but that does not decrease their
ability to be parents. My dad, for example, was wrong most of
the time when it came to discipline. He was always disciplining
us out of anger and not out of love to bring correction. Most
times, I was not sure what I was being disciplined for because I

could not ask, and if I did ask, it aggravated the problem even more. But that did not make him less of a parent. I did not honor my parents because they were perfect. I did because God gave them the position of father and mother.

God is the only one who does not make mistakes, so to rebel against my parents' authority was rebelling against God and their appointment to those positions over me. Again, Ephesians 6:2–3 says to "'Honor your father and mother,' which is the first commandment with promise: 'that may be well with you and you may live long on the earth.'"

The promise in this commandment is twofold. Verse 3 says, "that it may be well with you and you may live long on the earth." The word *well* is the root word for *prosperous*. Esteem your parents so that you will be prosperous and live long on this earth.

It is not in our power to promote ourselves. Joining with people who grumble and gripe about everything will not lift us higher. If you join with other children to badmouth, speak evil of, and find fault with your parents, you will end up cursing your own blessings.

We often miss the blessings in front of us because they looks like curses. Some people do not want their parents around them when they are among friends because they feel their parents do not measure up.

3 John 1:2 says, "Beloved, I pray that you may prosper in all things and be in health, just as your soul prospers." God gives us this promise when we obey his words, and that same

promise is given to children who obey, honor, value, and esteem their parents.

I heard of a girl who was in the company of some well-to-do kids in her school. It was a boarding school, and each time her mother came to visit her, she would inform her friends that her housemaid was coming to see her. She told them her mom was dead and her dad was a businessman who was always on the go.

She did not like her mother around her because she was uneducated and did not resemble the mothers of her other friends. She barely spent time with her mom when she came to visit. She communicated little with her mom and did not show love toward her when her mom was trying to show love toward her.

That is such a dishonor to her mother, her father, her family, and to God.

1 Peter 2:18 says, "Servants, be submissive to your masters with all fear, not only to the good and gentle, but also to the harsh." This is not fear in the sense of running away from them in disgust but fear in reverence. God is asking us to do the same thing—to be submissive to those who are around us. You will find out that the key in life, the secret to everything, is being submissive to God and to those God has placed over us. The greatest lesson to learn in life is that you will need to submit to those you don't like or to those you don't agree with. We are not to submit only to those who are good and gentle, but also to those who are harsh, wicked, and difficult to work or live with.

How come Satan will not leave when you tell him to leave? How come diseases will not leave when you say "leave"? Why are the things you don't want in your life still there? It's probably because you don't do what God is instructing you to do through your parents. And if you are not responding to the ones in authority over you, those under your authority will not bow to you.

When I worked at the mental health clinic in Norman, Oklahoma, as a therapist under supervision, I started off with a great boss. She was a people person and was patient in training new workers. Not long after, she assumed a new position and transferred out. Then our group was assigned a new boss who had just passed her licensure in social services. Gradually, the place became tense, and she started micromanaging. Personally, I think she had issues at home, which she carried in to work and damaged the beauty of the environment. I worked with her until I finally left to work for a reputable agency. I did not agree with most of her style of leadership, yet I honored her because she was my boss.

Sometimes we want to push such people aside, get rid of them, or avoid them. But we have to learn to submit to them and learn from them. They have a place of authority over us, even though we may not like them or agree with them. God has not called us to a perfect work; he has not called us to work at a place and be liked by people. He has called us to submit to them so that the power of God can change this imperfect world through us.

So when we look to God, fear him, and reverence him, it will go well with us. When we look at our parents, respect them, and reverence them, it will go well with us.

1 Peter 5:6 says, "Therefore humble yourselves under the mighty hand of God, that he may exalt you in due time." What is the mighty hand of God? It is your boss. It is your pastor. It is your supervisor. It could be the policeman who stopped you for going through the red light or for the speeding you denied.

When you have to face things in life you don't agree with, if you humble yourself under the mighty hand of God, he will exalt you in due time. We cannot see God with our physical eyes, but those around us represent God. By submitting to them, you are submitting to God.

You might say, "Yes, but my dad isn't God, and he is an unbeliever and wicked and does not deserve my submission, obedience, or honor." But God is saying, "If you can submit to me, if you can submit to them, I have a promotion waiting for you." Humble yourselves, therefore, under the mighty hand of God that he may exalt you in due time.

So God is saying that blessings come when we understand the simple things of submission. The mighty hand of God is the person above you—the person over you. When you submit, you set yourself up for promotion.

Young people at home, the way you submit to God is the way you submit to your parents. Again, Ephesians 6:1–3 says, "Children, obey your parents in the Lord, for this is right. 'Honor your father and mother,' which is the first command-ment with promise: 'that it may be well with you and you may live long on the earth.'"

In counseling, I hear a lot of kids say they have a good mother and father, that they are nice, and that they buy them everything. I have even heard some say, "My friend's mom and dad are nicer than my parents, so how do I act nice with them?"

I tell them, "That is too bad."

Welcome to life. We keep comparing parents, who is good and who is bad. That is life; life isn't fair.

Every time you want to do something, unfairness stares you in the face. It will be that way until Jesus comes. Only Jesus is fair. Only Jesus is understanding, and only Jesus is above all.

So submitting to those around you and your parents is God's plan for promotion; he calls it mercy. So, children, young people, learning to submit to your parents brings you great success, a long life, and well-being.

Your teachers at school, those who are over you—the administrators—whether you like them or not, whether they are nice or not, they represent God, so if you honor them and submit to them, you will be promoted, it will be well with you, and you will have a long life because learning to submit to authority is learning to submit to God. God says, "If you do that to them, and to your parents, then your blessing will come in due time because you have done it to me."

Your boss, the pastor of your church, your teachers—these are areas of life where God has placed us under authority, and we must offer respect to them. Your parents may not ask you to agree with everything they teach, and many of you will disagree with certain things they say, but that is not the issue. The issue is submission to those over you and having the correct attitude toward them. Remember that there may come a day when you will be called to lead your own family.

The way you treat your parents, pastors, and bosses will transfer to other areas of your life. Luke 16:12 says, "And if you have not been faithful in what is another man's, who will give you what is your own?" If you do not give your parents what is theirs, who will give you what is yours when you come of age? Remember, one good turn deserves another. It is possible that you are not living a blessed life because you have not joined God's program, which is to obey, and it will be well with you, and you will have a long life.

We have to understand that in asking God for anything, our priorities need to be right. If we do not have a life of integrity, a life of uprightness, or a life of obedience, why would God trust us with the riches we are asking for?

As a parent, you may be getting obedience out of your children, but you also have to teach them to honor you. If they honor you, they will live long on the earth, and things will go well with them. If you tell your son to take out the trash, he may obey you in your presence, but if he murmurs and complains all the way from the kitchen to the trashcan, he has dishonored you.

Your son or daughter may obey you when you give them a command, but what about when they talk back to you? What about when they say things in your face? That is dishonor. Scripture says that honoring is the first commandment with a promise, "that it may be well with you and you may live long on the earth." I want things to go well for my children.

If you want your children to live long, happy, successful, fulfilling, and blessed lives, then we have to teach them to obey and honor us as parents. The fifth commandment in Exodus 2 says "to honor your father and mother." Anyone who fails to do so will have trouble obeying all the other commandments.

Parents cannot be disengaged. You are raising your children in ungodly times. You should never be afraid to bring up your children in instruction and admonition. Satan never takes a break, and you should not take a break from parenting. There is never going to be a day in your life that you wake up and find that the world gave up, or that Satan gave up, and there is no more trouble. That is why as a parent, you cannot call it quits any day because of all the ungodliness and challenges you face in raising up children. Through the power of God, you can raise up godly children no matter what.

Parents are an epistle before their children to walk, talk, demonstrate, teach, and use the word of God to set guidelines in the home. And all a child must do is obey, and blessings start to flow in the child's life. If you don't teach your children, admonish them, and set guidelines for them to obey, you will provoke them to wrath. It does not come just for spiritual things; it also comes for physical things.

Again 1 Peter 5:5 says, "Likewise you younger people, submit yourselves to your elders. Yes, all of you be submissive to one another, and be clothed with humility, for 'God resists the proud, But gives grace to the humble.'" The *humble* are those who are submissive to authority, to those God has placed over them. *Elder* here is not referring to age; it is referring to those in authority over you. We all stand in different positions.

I visited some unchurched folks when their grandson invited me to pray with them. We had a great time together, I led them to Christ, and I invited them to church. To my surprise, they said they would not go to a church where they had to sit under a pastor who is younger than they are. They had missed the point. I told them the universal church is older than they are, and our church is just part of them. The church was here before they were, and it will be here after they meet the Lord in heaven.

What determines your future is not where you are now, but rather *your attitude* toward where you are right now. God blesses those with the proper attitudes. It is not your natural boss who is going to promote you; it is your spiritual boss, God. He will exalt you in due time when you quit griping and murmuring about your situation and learn to submit to his mighty hand.

# Chapter 8

# TRAINING IS FOR THE CHILD

Train up a child in the way he should go,
And when he is old he will not depart from it.

—Proverbs 22:6

THIS VERSE IS SAYING TO train children in the way of the Lord. Jesus said, "I am the way, the truth, and the life" (John 14:6). The way is Jesus Christ, the word of God, and no other way. There has not been any one book that teaches you how to instruct your child. No child came with a manual. The Bible is the standard book in raising and instructing your child.

Children left alone will bring shame to their parents. So while the children are young, parents need to get involved in instructing and admonishing them so that when they are old, they will not depart from what their parents taught them.

Lamentation 3:27 says, "It is good for a man to bear the yoke in his youth." A yoke is attaching yourself to something other than yourself, then submitting, cooperating, and being in one accord with what you have attached yourself to.

Jesus said in Matthew 11:29–30, "Take My yoke upon you, and learn from Me, for I am gentle and lowly in heart, and you will find rest for your souls. For My yoke is easy and My burden is light." Jesus is telling us not to be hooked to anything except him because life will be easier that way.

Successful Christians and families have learnt to submit to Jesus and humble themselves to his authority. It is okay for a child to cry and whine and have his diapers changed when he is a baby. But it is not okay for a child to whine and cry when he is older as if the world revolves around him.

I have seen a number of children in Walmart on multiple occasions crying and sobbing, trying to reach a piece of candy or a toy on the shelf while the parents just watch them cry and make a spectacle of themselves. The child wants to make the parents buy them candy, and many parents give in just to avoid embarrassment.

Other parents will take their child to Walmart and skip the candy and the toy aisles or will not take the child at all. Instead, tell them you are taking them but that you are not going to buy them a toy or a piece of candy. When you get there, repeat what you said to them. "No candy today," or "no toy today." Train them to hear your voice. Train them to know you mean what you say, and be a person of integrity in their eyes, not a parent who is easily provoked.

Bring the child to church, camp, and school, and teach him by telling him to do what is right. If you let him get his way, you teach him to scream louder when he does not get what he wants. Teach him to yoke with the Lord early.

Teach them to hear the word *no* and to deal with it. If you don't teach them early, they will use tantrums, fit, and tears to get their way.

There are many reasons why fathers and mothers abuse their children. It is mostly a pride problem, not an anger problem. Rather it is strife and self-centeredness in their hearts. They are angry at their kids for selfish reasons. They interrupted your ball game—self-centered. They embarrassed you in front of your friends—self-centered.

This verse does not say "teach them or spank them." It says, "train them." Train not only means to discipline them but also to show them. Training is not telling them what to do and not doing it yourself. Many parents tell their children what to do and not to do, but they do the direct opposite of what they instruct their children to do. There are lots of traits in your child that you can identify and say, "I am directly responsible for that." Many parents try to undo what they've done when things start falling apart. Oh, how I wish every parent would learn some things before having children. Thank God for his grace, which covers our tracks.

So again, the scripture says, "Train up a child in the way he should go, And when he is old, he will not depart from it." It says "the way"—there is a way required to train up the child. This is not the way of the school instructors, the day care center, the child psychologist, or the counselor.

The word *train up* means "to dedicate" or "to initiate." It means to set aside, to dedicate the child to God, which is something you would find in a church. When children are born, at a certain time we bring them to the church to be dedicated. That is what "train up a child" means—to bring the child to God to be trained by the word of God, which is "the way." When seeds of the word of God are sown in a child, it will remind him of the right way when he deviates from the norm.

God wants you, as a parent, to initiate so God can do a good work in your child's life. Parents have told me that it is too late for them to start training up their children in the word of God because they are in their teens and going through difficulty. I always tell them to just initiate and let Christ take over. They are in your home. They are a gift to you, and no one will take a gift from someone after it has been given. You will have to dedicate them before Christ can take over.

Parents, while they are in your home, you have to initiate/dedicate, and when they are gone, you can pray for them. They will meet other people who will help them find the path or rededicate themselves to God. So no matter what, there is a time in a child's life that you should dedicate or initiate. Your child may be challenged by the world's system, and you have to trust God that your initiation will work.

As they grow up, what your children believe will be put to the test. If they are disciplined in the word, they will stand on it and beat all odds that come their way. So as your child gets older, he will not depart from the way he is traveling. Aside from our physical walk, there is a spiritual walk we need to take in life. Moms and dads get to a point where they have no control over children as they grow. But if you train and turn them over to God, he knows how to continue to deal with them.

Many parents raise their children in the fear of the world instead of in the faith of God. The Bible teaches us that we are in the world but not of the world. We cannot lock our doors and avoid stepping out because we fear the world. We have to face the world each and every day. We have to be insulated and not isolated from it. We cannot live on an island with our children. Jesus said in John 16:33, "Be of good cheer, I have overcome the world." Do not teach your children to be fearful of the world; instead, teach them to have faith in God. This will help them not to be ruled or influenced by the world.

Paul said in 2 Timothy 1:5, "When I call to remembrance the genuine faith that is in you, which dwelt first in your grandmother Lois and your mother Eunice, and I am persuaded is in you also." What you don't have, you cannot pass on. What you don't have, you cannot give.

Paul is talking about genuine faith, strong faith, and faith that is reliable and worth having. He's not talking about some weak or unstable faith. You can only give what you have, so pass on genuine faith. He says, "Timothy, your faith is what was taught to your grandmother, and she taught it to your mother, who has also taught you this same genuine faith." So the question is, when did Timothy learn it? 2 Timothy 3:14–15 says:

> But you must continue in the things
> which you have learned and been assured of,
> knowing from whom you have learned them,

and that from childhood you have known the
Holy Scriptures, which are able to make you
wise for salvation through faith which is in
Christ Jesus.

So Timothy started learning it when he was a child. This
is the best time to instruct someone. However, you can start
instructing your child at any age. This verse encourages us to
pass on our faith from generation to generation. Never in our
lives do we have to be afraid of the works of the enemy or what
the world is planning against us. "He who is in you is greater
than he who is in the world" (John 4:4). There is no day that
Satan is more powerful that God. He can stop the local church,
but the universal church is forever. We are here as ambassadors
of God.

I was in my early twenties when I gave my life to Christ.
Recently, I had the opportunity to communicate with the guy
who helped me when I was a young believer. I sent several mes-
sages to him, but he never responded. I was told he has become
cold in the things of God, doing things he would normally not do.

I sent him a text, and he finally texted back. I thanked
him for all that he had done for me. He took me to nightly
prayer vigils, and I spent most of my mornings at his house.
And because both of us were available, we would get together,
pray, worship, and study the Bible.

While we were texting one another, he said, "Oh my,
Pastor, I am happy you have kept the faith and are currently

enroute to God. I am here, too, in the faith but not on fire as you are."

I responded, "That is okay. I will remember you always in my prayers."

Just do your part faithfully. God is with you. I have initiated him back by letting him know I am praying for him. Again, our children can live in the world and not fall to the temptations of the world.

It is important for parents to instruct and discipline their children as God instructs and disciplines us, by his word. 2 Timothy 3:16–17 says, "All scripture is given by inspiration of God, and it's profitable for doctrine, for reproof, for correction, for correction in righteousness."

One powerful tool is to learn to say *no*. Your children should not suffer for a rule they do not know, even in the word of God. God does not hold sins we are not aware of against us. He holds us accountable for the sins we do know. Children should be disciplined when they break a rule they know about.

Parents, learn to trust your children from a very young age. It is a good thing to have trust in God and in your children. 3 John 4 says, "I have no greater joy than to hear that my children walk in truth." From the time they are young, trust them to choose things for themselves. When our daughter entered high school, we made her choose which classes she wanted to take. And she did very well in all her classes. As your children grow, give them some latitude. If they were out longer than you told them to be, don't get all rough with them; ask for an explanation.

It is also okay to allow your children to be themselves while you still tell them you trust them to make the best choices they can. Allow your children to be part of their generation without being controlled by it. Stop making your children dress as though they are part of your generation. Let them choose what they wear, but exercise your authority to approve their outfits.

*Chapter 9*

# SET THE COURSE FOR YOUR CHILD

And you, fathers, do not provoke your children<br>
to wrath, but bring them up in the training<br>
[nurture] and admonition of the Lord.

—Ephesians 6:4

THE WORD *NURTURE* MEANS MORE than to nourish, feed, train, or discipline. The word *admonition* means "mild instructions." In other words we are to provide the kind of care that will promote healthy growth and development, which includes discipline in love. This deals with spiritual and moral development that flows out of a right relationship with God. *Nurture* refers to that environment in which children are to be raised that brings together, like a corral gate, all the sides and ingredients for the training corral. Parents have a command to discipline and instruct their children in the Lord.

This is not a job to be done by the daycare assistant or your state agency. Agencies have interfered with the rights of parents for far too long. Parents should understand that discipline should be backed by instruction. They should teach the children why they should go a certain way and instruct them to do so.

Punishment is not discipline. Punishment is what it is: punishment. The challenge is most parents never establish or identify a goal when it comes to discipline. They discipline out of anger or to reciprocate the effects of the wrong the child did. Is it possible for parents to know the right way to discipline their children in each given situation? No! But with grace and patience, and with the right attitude, we can do the right thing.

God calls our children *arrows* and calls us parents *warriors*. They are in our hands, not in the hands of the daycare or the government. One day we are going to launch them or send them out of our home to a challenging, dark, and perverted world. We as parents have to prepare them to be launched out of our quiver.

Ephesians 6:4 says, "And you, fathers, do not provoke your children to wrath, but bring them up in the training and admonition of the Lord." Children are provoked when you discipline them without telling them why. It is important that we are not disciplining our children for our own ego or image, but for them. We need to instruct them from the word of God why we are disciplining them so they will not be provoked.

Colossians 3:21 says, "Fathers, do not provoke your children, lest they become discouraged." Parents can damage their children by disciplining them with no understanding. I remember one church where I first joined the choir. We had an opportunity to record a demo on the importance of breastfeeding. After the demo was played for us, I realized that something did not sound right. Out of the eight of us in the room, who were the singers, my pastor singled me out, and in the presence of everyone, he said, "Michael, you messed up the recording." I walked out of the place and never wanted to be part of it, only to find out it was some feedback problem.

His statement devastated me, and I admit my actions were out of place, even though I did not say a word to him. I left the group for about a week before calming down and returning. I was discouraged and hurt, but I got over it. The challenge was I did not have anybody at that time to give me scripture to curb my pain and discouragement. When I did not return, no one called me to see how I was doing.

Scripture makes it emphatically clear that the father's primary role at home is to train and discipline the children, to be the head of the home. The mother's primary role is to help raise the children and to keep the home. Children are to be raised not in anger, not in abuse, and not in wrath or punishment, but in loving discipline and counsel that brings the revelation of our Lord. When we point them to the discipline of the Lord, when they are no longer under our roof but on their own, they will respond properly to the correction from their heavenly Father.

My motive is to discipline, not punish, them, not to inflict pain, not to use excessive force, and not to hurt them. The point is not to "do something to them" so they can learn a lesson, but to help them correct their faults so Jesus can be seen in them. Fathers correct according to Hebrews 12:9 and not punish. Punishment has wrath with it. Punishment has retributions with it. Punishment has pain associated with it.

Many parents do not respond right to discipline, mostly because discipline in their home was bad. Either they had an abusive dad, a runaway dad, or disengaged dad. They were in some way mishandled by their natural father, so it is difficult for them to relate to their heavenly Father. So, the way they handle their children leads to provocation of anger. It causes their children to blow up and fuss and not respond properly to their discipline and training. James 1:20 says, "for the wrath of man does not produce the righteousness of God." Your anger will not produce the results God will want to see in your children.

It's a myth to think nothing is going to change unless you get angry, put your foot down, or raise your voice. It will bring change but not a healthy change. I saw my dad do that. It was not fun, and it did not produce the righteousness of God. He loved to correct situations as they arose but could not always discipline rightly. At times, I am sure he disciplined just for the fun of it, unable to let things go.

In my parenting, I was emulating those same old ways, producing unhealthy changes until I realized God wants me to treat my children the way he treats me—with love and affection. God does not scream at me to see change. He does not get angry at me to bring change, and he does not have to put his foot down to see change in me.

I was recently talking to two of my younger brothers, who are pastors, and I asked them if they had any memory of our dad's discipline. Jake said he remembers a Sunday morning when he woke up not feeling well and did not want to go to church, and he and Frederick were made to stay home. After a few hours, they decided to go pluck some oranges by the side of the house about thirty meters away. He said he was on the orange tree when my dad came back from church. Noticing him on the orange tree and Fredrick underneath it, our dad asked who was there, and Jake pretended it was someone else.

He added that my dad told him to get down or he would be stoned. Before he could get down from the tree, my dad had already started releasing pebbles into the tree, hitting him from all angles. That was not fun, and it did not produce the righteousness of God.

Avoiding disciplining your children when you're angry means looking at them and saying, "I am out of control. My flesh has kicked in. Anything I do now would be unbearable and un-Christian. I am angry, and if I discipline you at this moment, I might not do it out of love. So, here is what we are going to do. I am going to spank you, and I am going to discipline you. But I am going to pray about it. I am going to wait on God. And I am going to sleep on it, and you need to do the same." How many of you realize that this waiting time is just as powerful as spanking?

Another way we provoke our children is by physically or verbally abusing them. Even excessive spanking leaves marks. Never spank too young, too old, too hard, and too much. We spank our children unto correction to teach them right, not unto abuse. Done right, it demonstrates love that delivers our children from wrong and for a season. Proverbs 22:15 calls it the rod of correction, not the rod of wrath. Proverbs 29:15 calls it the rod of reproof and instruction, not the rod of wrath.

Spanking that does not produce reproof and correction defeats the purpose.

A lot of parents I have observed, talked to, and met in counseling do not spank their children, but curse them, called them names, label them as "good for nothing," or wish death and defeat over them. Some apply the anger and resentment they have for their own mothers and fathers, which only transfers hate and shame to the children. I once heard a mother say to her son, "You, I should have sat on your head when you were coming out of me." I heard another say, "I would have stopped pushing you out if I knew this is what you were going to turn out to be." Children are a blessing to parents, yet parents can provoke them to anger.

Ephesians 4:29 says, "Let no corrupt word proceed out of your mouth, but what is good for necessary edification, that it may impart grace to the hearers. " This verse says that we as parents, even in our discipline, need to encourage our children. We need to edify them, love them, and show them grace. We need grace from God when we are wrong, and they need grace when they mess up. That self-righteous thing parents do as though they have never messed up before is condescending and condemning. God does not condemn us to change our behavior. He shows us more and more grace.

Speak politely to them, not mean, not loud, not harsh, and not dirty. Don't rain curse words on them. God wants us to do for them what we want done for us. Remember all the times you got into trouble when you were their age?

Inconsistency also leads to provocation and anger. Discipline your children when they are wrong, not when you're angry. If you have mood swings, check them before you discipline. Discipline is for correction, not about how you, the parent, feel. Rule your house with love and affection.

In many homes, the child is always asking, "What did I do?" Many children do not know what they get in trouble for. That can provoke them to anger. Parents need to make it clear to the child what they did wrong and the consequences they face. Children react in genuine repentance and awareness when they know what they did and not wonder why they are being punished for something they did not do. They will produce resistance, fussing, and bellyaching over your authority.

Do not discipline in public or in front of peers. Your children will spew resentment toward you and, one day, toward God. Some fathers and mothers will go to their children's school to sit in class with them to embarrass them for having bad grades. Do you really expect them to concentrate and bring home good grades if you're sitting in there with them? Discipline is not about disgracing or embarrassing your child. It is not about shaming your child, making him feel guilty or condemned.

If you do not want to have shame, do not give birth to a child because that is what children do. Adam and Eve had the best dad—God himself. He visited them in the cool of the day. See, any name Adam gave to the animals, trees, and anything else, God responded positively to it, and it was so. God never said, "Let us make animals in our image and have dominion over the earth."

When God made animals, he knew in his mind what they should look like. But when he made man, he himself was the image. He looked in the mirror and said, "That is what man should look like—the exact image and resemblance," yet Adam and Eve disobeyed their perfect Father. How much more will our children disobey us?

God, not wanting them to eat the tree of life, sent them out of the garden in love. God has never corrected you publicly; he never corrected anyone publicly in the Bible. He punished them publicly so that anyone who sees it will learn and be corrected. Don't correct your children publicly.

Do not show favoritism and the favoritism that provokes to anger. Do not treat one child better than the other. Do not punish one harder than the other. Do not do stuff with one and then ignore the others. Do not buy new clothing for one and send the others to the thrift store.

Genesis 37:4 says, "But when his brothers saw that their father loved him more than all his brothers, they hated him and could not speak peaceably to him." Jacob made Joseph, not the other boys, a coat of many colors. He showed Joseph more love than the other boys. They saw this and could not manage their anger toward him. Jacob provoked the other boys to anger by demonstrating his excessive love for Joseph. Favoritism can be seen in a godly home and in blended families.

Comparing your children with other children to put them down can provoke children to anger. Many parents, in the bid to get their children to do well, are always comparing them to other people's children. Let me be your alarm clock—everyone's child has a problem. Recently, I was talking to a family about their child and how she was a gracious young girl, and they said to me, "You don't know her, Pastor. She needs counseling to come out of the evil she does." I was scared.

You can be too strict with your children. Parents drive their children away from God and away from relationships. Acts 15:10 says, "Now therefore, why do you test God by putting a yoke on the neck of the disciples which neither our fathers nor we were able to bear?" This scripture is saying, "Why in the world did we put all this laws upon the Gentiles even our fathers could not keep? We know it is impossible for us to keep them, and yet we expect them to keep them."

Check and see all the limitations and boundaries you put on your child; some cannot be met. Children are humans, not spirits, and they live on the earth. Failing is an event; being a failure is a condition. There is a difference between failing and being a failure. Just because you have been failing or just because you failed does not mean you are a failure. Failing is part of the human condition. Some of us are too cautious of failing, and because of that, we will not try anything at all. Humans make mistakes; we fail and must be treated with grace. Children make mistakes and must be met with grace.

Children hate to see the fathers physically abusing their mothers. Many children will fight back if they get the opportunity or if they are of age. I know many children who have attacked their fathers for abusing their mothers. What a shame for a child to fight a parent. Children who cannot or do not fight will despise you shamefully. They will wish they did not have to stay with you, and they will wish they were out of your home.

Again, Ephesians 6:4 says, "And you, fathers, do not provoke your children to wrath, but bring them up in the training and admonition of the Lord." We are to bring our children up in the nurture and admonition of the Lord. The word *nurture* means "discipline, correction, chasten, or chastisement." The word *admonition* means "mild rebuke." It means calling attention to. It means instruction; it means teaching.

A mild rebuke is, "No, don't do that," "No, don't touch it," or "No, don't go there; it's not a good place." When you do not teach your children, and you do not discipline your children in time, you provoke them to wrath. We have an entire generation full of anger and wrath because they were not taught what is right and wrong and were not made to conform to certain standards. So they have no discipline or control in their lives, so they respond with wrath.

When we do not teach our children and when we do not discipline our children, we provoke them to anger. Children need boundaries; children need rules. They want to know where the lines are in the sand and be held accountable. If you fail to teach and admonish your children and set guidelines for them to obey, you will provoke them to wrath. You cannot ask your child to do what you have not taught them. Parents, not only should you show your child what to do, but you should also show them how to do it.

# Chapter 10

# A WORD FOR FATHERS AND MOTHERS

My son, keep your father's command,
And do not forsake the law of your mother.

—Proverbs 6:20

How MANY OF YOU KNOW that if you want to live for God, then you have to live for God with everything you have? If you want to be married then you put everything into it to make the marriage work. If you want to do business, then you put everything into it to make the business work. If you want to sing, then you put everything into it to be able to sing well. If you want to preach, you have to put every effort into it to make it work.

So it is with raising children. If you want to raise kids, then you put everything into the process to make the parenting work so you don't raise ill-mannered kids. We all know what we want the future for our kids to be. But in all this, there is a process. Without the process, getting there becomes the issue. Christ knew he had to go to the cross, but he understood there was no other process to go to the cross than "O My Father, if it is possible, let this cup pass from Me…" (Matthew 26:39). Your process is different from mine. To some of us, there is no other way, but to trust and obey God in our process.

The problem with most of us as Christian parents is that we do not allow ourselves to be rooted in a place or in the process of parenting. We do not give the word of God a chance in our lives. God's word is a seed. When you sow a seed, you don't just walk off and expect a harvest the next day. You do a lot with that seed you just planted. You weed around it, you keep bugs off it, you water it, you fertilize it, and you give it time and patience to grow.

Whatever God promises us or says about us is true, but we have a part to play to become the people we need to become. Jesus never promised there would be no challenges. In fact he said, "I will be with you when you go through the water. I will be with you when you go through the fire"—how long I do not know. But I trust what Psalm 23:4 says: "Yea, though I walk through the valley of the shadow of death, I will fear no evil; For You are with me; Your rod and Your staff, they comfort me."

This scripture says, "the valley of the shadow." A shadow is not real. That means it is not the real thing. It is just the shadow. At the appearance of light, which is his word, the shadow will disappear. No one said parenting is easy. Variations of shadows seem to make parenting difficult: kids don't listen, they don't do what you think is right, they defy you, and they embarrass you. All this seems real, but they are not the main thing. When you go to the source of parenting, which is the word of God, you will have light. You will have insight to accomplish what the word is designed to accomplish, and this is by his grace and staying with the process. So, in my process, I have to learn to trust and have faith in God.

I hear people say, "If you are not coming with me, then I am not going." Jeremiah 1:5 says, "Cursed is the man who trusts in man and makes flesh his strength…" If you are a Christian, you must not be content until you develop the full potential the Lord has given you. That is how you bring glory to God.

Your attitude toward life, your consecration in service, and your abundant love will lift you above the average parent. If you decide to live above average, God will bypass all the people around you, above you, and beneath you to bring his purposes to pass in your life. Your parenting cannot be better than you as a person.

Parents are from God, and the ability to parent is also from God. Anything from him is good and perfect. God has no problems interjecting in anything he gives. There is no such thing as a parenting problem because parenting comes from God, and God does not give anything that has problems. Salvation comes from God, and there is no problem attached to it.

In order to do this parenting thing well, you have to go to the source, and the key to keep growing in parenting is to continue steadfastly despite what people say, despite circumstances, despite adversity, despite demons, and despite what the children reciprocate.

The strength in parenting comes from unity. When parents rises up in unity, that is when the gates of hell are defeated. We love to create separations among us as parents. We keep magnifying our differences and weaken our efforts to win. When we get together in the Holy Spirit, we find out that we have more in common than we did in our differences. Unity is key among parents, and if you are a single parent, or a guardian, you need to be in unity with the word of God and the Holy Spirit.

Matthew 12:25 says, "But Jesus knew their thoughts, and said to them: "Every kingdom divided against itself is brought to desolation, and every city or house divided against itself will not stand." Jesus starts with the large and proceeds down to the small. He starts with kingdoms, then goes down to cities, and finally to the house.

The kingdom here can be the spiritual or the natural one. The principles that work here in the spiritual also work in the natural. The same principles work in the home. Anyone who can run the home can run the nation. That is why the Bible says he that cannot take care of his household, how can he take care of the church?

The same thing that is true for a church is true for the home. What Jesus is speaking here is the power of unity. Disunity is what causes the home to be divided. Unity is what will keep a city and a kingdom from being divided. Strength comes from unity.

The greatest power you have is unity. A husband and a wife agreeing together is powerful, and they have a good reward for their labor. For God has made them one together in heart, one together in flesh, and one together in spirit. Therefore, togetherness is powerful. The more we are unified, the more Satan is divided.

David had two sons, Absalom and Adonijah. Both of them ended up in rebellion and death because they did not listen to, nor were they properly instructed by, their parents. But David and Bathsheba got together and instructed Solomon in the word of God, and Solomon became a great parson, a great king, and a great blessing.

Children are to be the builders of the family name, not the destruction of it. The way they build on the family name is to take the instruction their parents teach them and continue building on the family name generation after generation. That is God's plan for us as his people: to become wiser generation after generation, to be prosperous generation after generation, and to do his will generation after generation.

My parents were lay preachers in the church they attended, and today four of their children are minsters of the gospel, and every one of us is active in church. All of our children are in church as well and playing a role in advancing the kingdom. We are building the family name generation to generation. That is how it should be in our lives.

Notice in Proverbs 6:20, "My son, keep your father's command, And do not forsake the law of your mother," that the husband, the father, is the one who has the commandment. The mother, the wife, has the law. The word *commandment* means "discipline, correction"—it is the father who disciplines. The mother can discipline too, but God has put the primary role of discipline on the father.

The word *law* there means "precepts and teachings." It is the mother who is responsible primarily for the precepts and teachings of the children. It is the mother whom God called to be home with the children, raising and rearing them in their formative years.

It is the husband's primary role to provide. Husbands have to work; wives get to work. The husband is the provider of the home; the wife is the guide of the home. The father is the commander, he is the head, he is the overseer, and he is the disciplinarian. If he says, "I want the living room cleaned by the time I come home from work at 5 p.m." then Mama is the one who guides, teaches, and instructs the child in how it should be done. That is the role of the mother.

Many people have heard the word *discipline* applied to a good marriage and rearing children but have not done it. James 1:23–25 teaches that if you are a hearer of the word and not a doer, you deceive yourself. The blessings are not in the hearing, but in the doing.

When we train our children, the training is passed on from them to their children and on and on. Just because you are good, that does not grantee your child will be good. Just because you are rich, that does not mean your child will be rich. You have to teach those things to them.

One day, your children are going to come out from your home and from under your authority. When they reach a certain age and start paying their own rent and bills, you will not be able to stop them from staying out late. You will not be able to command them to obey you because they are adults. But they must seek to honor you as long as you live.

One way they honor us is that everywhere they go, they remember the teachings, precepts, and law of their mother. And everywhere they go, they remember the discipline of their father. In their minds, they hear "Don't do that, or there will be consequences."

I have never known anyone or read about anyone who has prospered without discipline. We need to teach our children delayed gratification from the time they are toddlers. We have not taught them what not to do. We have not taught our children to stay away from drugs, sexual perversion, and sinful communication. Instead we have made excuses for them. "Oh, he is a child and knows nothing. He or she will grow out of it." Teach them to wait their turn and help them learn when and where not to do certain things. Discipline and training are not fun, but if you keep at it constantly, you will see progress.

Proverbs 29:15 says, "The rod and rebuke give wisdom, But a child left to himself brings shame to his mother." If you put off disciplining your child, the results are going to be grievous in their later days, and you will regret missing the opportunity. I know a couple who has two little children. These children are allowed to do anything they choose to—draw on the walls, spit at each other, and run around the house as late as 11:00 p.m. I asked them why they sleep late, and they told me they just don't want to go to bed early. Children are children. They need boundaries and direction, and parents need to teach and instill structure in them. Sometimes the rod of correction should be introduced.

Proverbs 22:15 says, "Foolishness *is* bound up in the heart of a child; The rod of correction will drive it far from him." Foolishness is bound in a Baptist child. It is bound in a

Pentecostal child. It is bound in a lost man's child. It's bound in a saved man's child. It is bound in the pastor's child. It is bound in the teacher's child. But the rod of correction will drive it far from him.

The rod of correction is not the rod of child abuse. The rod of correction is not the rod of anger. The rod of correction is not the rod of wrath, and the rod of correction is not the rod of hatred. It is the rod of love to bring correction and redirection to the child.

The rod of correction is the rod of reproof. A child cannot read. A child cannot understand. But if he will be obedient to the word of God that his parents are teaching him, the same blessings that come to the adult will come to the child—a road to prosperity and a road to long life on this earth.

To some parents it is the reproach your children have brought to you that has caused you to hold grudges and not forgive them. Forgiveness is God's extended love for you.

Forgiveness is God proving his love for you. He did not just say he loves you. He proved it to you by forgiving you. Romans 5:8 says, "But God demonstrates His own love toward us, in that while we were still sinners, Christ died for us." Your forgiveness toward your child is God's extended love through you.

Forgiveness does not excuse the actions of our children. Forgiveness stops their actions from destroying your heart. It hurts, but how long would you demand that your child come to beg you for forgiveness before you forgive? Some of us parents are still holding stuff over our children, wanting them to prove themselves before we mend our relationship with them. That is why they are still not coming home. Start getting right with them. Stop getting even with them.

The parable of the lost son in Luke 15:20b says, "but when he was still a great way off, his father saw him and had compassion, and ran and fell on his neck and kissed him." It was the father who chose to forgive his son in his heart before his son ever came home. He hated what that boy had done, but he was not condemning him. Even though the father was disappointed and angry, he did not take it out on the son. Look for the opportunity to talk about the matter and move on. It might be uncomfortable, but you need to share how you feel.

We should not be rude to our children. We must forgive so Satan will not take advantage of us. We can forgive them first when they wrong us and then repair the relationship.

# Chapter 11

# RAISING A WISE SON OR DAUGHTER

Unless the LORD builds the house,
They labor in vain who build it;
Unless the LORD guards the city,
The watchman stays awake in vain.
It is vain for you to rise up early,
To sit up late,
To eat the bread of sorrows;
For so he gives His beloved sleep.
Behold, children are a heritage from the LORD,
The fruit of the womb is a reward.
Like arrows in the hand of a warrior,
So are the children of one's youth.
Happy is the man who has his quiver full of them;
They shall not be ashamed,
But shall speak with their enemies in the gate.

—Psalm 127:1–5

WE SEE FROM THIS PASSAGE that except the Lord build the house, they who labor, labor in vain. Have you ever started something and could not finish it because you did not know what you were doing and did not refer to the manual? The first thing to understand is that to raise functional children—wise children—we need the Lord.

When you do not know the purpose of a thing, you may abuse or misuse it, and by the time you figure out what it's for, you may have destroyed it. Again, parents need to understand that to raise functional children—wise children—we need the Lord. Parenting never rises above the levels of the individuals in the marriage.

Your parenting will never be better than you are as an individual. Your parenting is a reflection of your relationship with God. If someone were to examine your parenting, would it be a great reflection of your relationship with God or a reflection of who you really are? Your passion toward the things of life must first begin with you passion toward God. Just as God has done for you, he will begin to do for your children. He will pour himself into them.

The Lord is the source of your understanding. The greatest gifts you can give your children is a father who loves their mother with the love that she wants and a mother who reverences the father with the kind of reverence he wants.

Proverbs 14:12 says, "There is a way that seems right to a man, But its end is the way of death." The world has a way of doing things, and God's people have a way of doing things. The two are never the same: one leads to destruction, and the other leads to righteousness and life. So we need to receive instruction from the Lord on how to raise our children.

Parents need to point their children in the right direction, so when they are shot out of the quiver, they can hit their target through discipline, through teaching, and through instruction. They may wobble a bit, and they may falter a bit, but once we point them in the right direction, they can hit the target of holiness and godliness, and we will rejoice.

Start teaching and discipling your children early God's word. Get your children in church in their early years. Get them in Sunday school. Get them in extracurricular activities that are beneficial to them. Don't leave them wandering and making friends you do not know. Start becoming friends with them early and let them gain confidence in you.

My wife has a thing with our children. She tells them, "Anytime someone tells you a secret, share it with me so I can tell you if it is okay to keep." Let them know they can trust you. It is never too late to get them into the word of God. The first five years are the formative years of their lives, so stop behaving like other parents: "They are still young. They need time to grow and understand." Just because you know something that does not mean they will know it. Teach it to them.

Many parents are not involved in the lives of their children. Many parents disengage when they hit a rock in their effort to train their child. We have to get involved in their lives, and it takes sacrifice. If you leave your child to the world, he will be influenced by society and the wrong crowd. Parents, you have to pay now and play later. You have to know your kids and participate in what they like. Go to their games, dances, and activities. Be part of their daily lives.

To raise a wise child, expose them to consequences. Do not shield your children from the repercussions of their actions. Hebrews 12:6 says, "For whom the LORD loves He chastens…" You are not doing them any favors by letting them do something wrong and letting it go or covering it up.

The worst teaching our children face is when an adult does something wrong and does not get punished for it. Driving with your child, you run through red lights and laugh at it. You break the rule and get away with it. While the father is the first example a child may have at home, the mother may be the first example to the child. Children learn what they see. Parents are the examples the child will learn from. Your children need to be disciplined when they do wrong, and they need to see others disciplined when they do wrong.

You have to guide their company. When our sons were growing up, we were careful of the friends they had. Some of their friends' parents we knew through teachers' days and PTA meetings, and some lived in the neighborhood. Some friends who showed up to play games we had never met before. Our boys loved sleepovers, and we let them have them, but it was all done in our home. We encouraged their friends to come and sleep over at our house, rather than our children going to sleep in other people's homes. Let others spend a night in your house and stop letting your children run around in other people's homes when you do not know who the people are. Do not be suspicious of every friend your children has, but do not be oblivious to signs and intuitions. Be alert and ready to intervene or possibly stop the friendship in love.

Proverbs 13:20 says, "He who walks with wise men will be wise, But the companion of fools will be destroyed." Some of you parents are pulling your hair out because of your children. If you have teenagers, make your house the hangout. You might have to check the games they play, the music they listen to, and the crowd they hang out with, and you might have to cast out the scorner.

You do not know what other parents allow their children to do. You do not know what is on their computers and what restrictions they have. Have the children in your house and show them what a Godly home looks like. Let them see how you and your family conduct yourselves. It might be a starting point for the other children to learn. Use your manners and be polite in your conversations.

To raise wise sons and daughters, parents have to have wisdom. First of all, wisdom comes from God, and you can receive it if you ask for it, in line with his word and according to his promises. We stand in faith and ask. We stand on his word and ask for wisdom, and God grants it to us. James 1:5 says, "If any of you lacks wisdom, let him ask of God, who gives to all liberally and without reproach, and it will be given to him." We also have the example of Solomon asking for wisdom, and it was granted him. Many of us fail to recognize, however, that wisdom is not gained when you are old and gray. It starts in the womb. As the child begins to grow, wisdom begins to form in them as people around him guide him in it and speak it to him.

Luke 2:52 says, "And Jesus increased in wisdom and stature, and in favor with God and men." He did not just become wise when he was grown; he grew in it. When he was twelve years old, he continued to submit to his heavenly Father, while he continued to submit to his earthly mom and dad. Jesus not only obeyed his parents; he showed respect for his mother, even while he was on the cross.

Children do not come to this earth with wisdom—that is why they need Mom and Dad, and that is why they need proper training, nurturing, admonition, and boundaries to guide them. Therefore, it is up to the parents to provide the foundation of wisdom for the child. It starts with the word of God. Proverbs 9:10 says, "The fear of the LORD is the beginning of wisdom…" Children are not fully grown. That is why parents should guide their company and provide a good home for them to thrive.

When children come to this earth and get born again, that is when the favor starts. The more they understand, apply God's word, submit to authority, and submit to their parents, the more they increase in favor with God and with men.

There are things in a family we should all be aware of so we can conduct ourselves properly in our daily lives. Man received a curse on his occupation after disobeying God in Genesis. If a man does not rely on the word of God or the power of God, certain things in life will not go well. The nature of the flesh takes over. With the woman, we find out there was a curse in childbearing and raising up children, and women need to turn to the word of God and the power of God to learn not to usurp men's authority.

If the man has a curse on him and the woman also has a curse, what about the child? Yes, Proverbs 22:15 tells us that "Foolishness is bound up in the heart of a child; The rod of correction will drive it far from him." It says the rod of correction, not the rod of abuse. This is something a child needs to overcome and parents need to overcome. Man, by himself, has no goodness in him. Remove God from a man, and man can be a dangerous creature, a sinner, an enemy, wicked, and evil. Jeremiah 17:9 says, "The heart is deceitful above all things, And desperately wicked; Who can know it?" Who can know what a man is thinking at any given time?

So we cannot leave children alone thinking they will become good people. It takes the finished work of Christ in our lives and applying the word of God to get us out of the curse. A lot of children fall victim to the curse because they do not have role models at home—Dad is doing his thing, and Mom is doing her thing. Each one is looking to the other to bring change, and the children are left to themselves.

Because the children are left to do their own thing, the foolishness begins to rise up and bloom into a tree of death and destruction. Children, in many cases, have been allowed to go their own way. Children needs boundaries, and what causes the boundaries to be removed is when Mom and Dad are doing their own thing and are out of fellowship with God. Parents are to set the boundaries, and that is when the safety and protection comes for children to grow up in the right way.

Proverbs 22:15 says, "Foolishness is bound up in the heart of a child." Foolishness is when a child is growing up and he has to have a good time. He has to be a happy person. But when the barriers are removed, he goes all the way into foolishness. These are children who do not have the proper protection and guidelines, and they may end up as the ones who love simplicity, the scorners who delight in their scorning, and fools who hate knowledge. They may end up in drugs, drinking, sex, and all forms of evil. Because foolishness is bound in their hearts, they run past having a good time and head into the curse. That is why God warns us they have to be kept in line. In the natural, they are kept in line with the rod. That is why Proverbs 22:15 also says, "The rod of correction will drive it far from him."

With that, there must be the constant instruction of the word of God. That is why children are to be raised in the nurture and admonition of the Lord. Nurture is discipline, and admonition is the teaching of God's word, and the two must go hand in hand to see results.

The difficulty today is that only a small percentage of children live in a traditional family, where the mother and the father are both in the house, where the father is the breadwinner, and where the mother is the trainer and raiser of the children. There are certain aspects of life that only a mother can teach a child, and there are other aspects only a father can teach.

Christian families need to have a constant relationship with the Lord and the word. The world today is bombarding families with a lot of lies and mocking what traditional families ought to look like. Christians are joining in on social media and other news outlets, laughing at the world's mockery of the traditional family, and that is what the world's aim is—to get Christians to join in and come along with them.

Again, Ephesians 6:1–4 says, "Children, obey your parents in the Lord, for this is right. 'Honor your father and mother,' which is the first commandment with promise: 'that it may be well with you and you may live long on the earth.' And you, fathers, do not provoke your children to wrath, but bring them up in the training and admonition of the Lord." In the first three verses, we have the submission of the child, and in the fourth verse, we have the submission of the parents.

Ephesians 5:21 says, "submitting to one another in the fear of God." This is not just parents submitting one to another, but parents submitting to their children. Through the infilling of the Holy Spirit, we learn when it is proper to submit to one another. There are times that we need to listen to what our children have to say. Sometimes a child can lead us in the right direction.

I remember in my own life, many years ago, my younger brother and I had an acre of land on a stretch of a road. A friend of our father wanted a fourth of it, and we gladly gave it to him so he would help us develop the other three. We were informed he had taken another piece without our knowledge. On our way to demolish and cover up what he was doing, we were met by a little boy about ten years old, who said to us, "Don't do it." We did not heed his warning, and we ended up in jail for about six hours for demolition.

Most parents from the Diaspora cannot submit to their children, even to listen to what they have to say. They have placed culture before the word of God—even those who are Christians—which has caused a lot of tension at home. Most live in other countries and behave as though they are in their mother country and get themselves into trouble with the law. It is proper to listen to what our children have to say.

The process of a child growing up begins with the child learning to obey his parents, and that is what is brought up in this scripture. It is a command. It is the responsibility of the child to obey, and parents also have the responsibility to listen to what the child has to say. This is what eventually causes our family and homes to become powerful on this earth.

Ephesians 6:1, however, is different from Ephesians 5:21: "Submitting to one another in the fear of God." This is husbands and wives submitting to one another. The word *submit* simply means "to align yourself under or be in line with." Or, as Ephesians 5:22 says, "Wives, submit to your own husbands, as to the Lord."

Children must align themselves under the authority of their parents or others who have authority over them and listen to them. Then Ephesians 6:2 says, "Honor your father and mother," which is the first commandment with promise. The word *honor* is to reverence or to have an attitude that backs up your obedience.

It was said of a young man who accompanied his mom to church that during the reading of the word, the entire congregation stood up for the readings because it was their culture. When the first scripture was being read, the young man did not stand. His mother beckoned him to, but he did not. During the reading of the second scripture, he still did not stand as all the others did. When the reading of the third scripture began, his mom asked him to stand for the reading, and he was still sitting. He turned to his mom and said, "You know, I do not want to be here. You made me. And even if I stand, I will still be sitting in my heart." Standing is depicting outward obedience, but the attitude was without honor.

Children are not to honor their parents because they are perfect and great at all things and never miss a beat. All parents are human, and human beings make mistakes. You honor them because of their position.

Honor doesn't stop with Mom and Dad; honor goes on throughout life. You are to honor your pastor and those who have positions in the church—the associate pastors, music directors, worship leaders, and so forth—because of the positions they hold. You honor your boss and anyone else in authority because of their position. You honor people who are in positions of authority, despite the fact that they make mistakes. One day, you are going to be a mom or a dad, and you will make mistakes too.

One day, you leave home to start your own family, but you continue honoring and listening to your parents. Proverbs 1:8 says, "My son, hear the instruction of your father, And do not forsake the law of your mother." This is a command and a decision a child has to make. Mom and Dad can speak, but the child has to make the effort to hear.

Revelation 3:22 says, "He who has an ear, let him hear what the Spirit says to the churches." To hear, we must choose to hear. If we don't choose to hear, we won't hear. Some people will not listen to you because they choose not to hear. You cannot get right with your kids by howling at them. You can't get righteousness into your children by being angry at them and calling that "talking." In fact, you cannot have any healthy communication with your children when you are being contentious with them.

You have control over how you speak to your child, but you don't have control of whether they hear you. So Mom and Dad can speak, and the child has to make the decision to hear.

This comes back to obedience. "My son, hear the instruction of your father, And do not forsake the law of your mother."

Proverbs 2:1a says, "My son, if you receive my words." This means to hear, discipline, and open yourself up. Don't just hear the words being said; listen to them, incline your ears to them, and understand them. It is very important to listen intently to what Mom and Dad are saying and receive the teaching.

We all know that children do not want to do what is right in the natural—clean their room, brush their teeth, and eat their vegetables. If it is not good, why eat it? Why spend all that time under a shower? If something takes too much time and they do not understand it, they do not want to do it. You give them medications, and they flush them down the toilet or sneak their food under the table and give it to the dog. They don't understand why these things are important, but if Mom and Dad say they are important, they have to treat them as important. With time, walking them through and helping them to learn and understand why certain things are important, one day they will thank you for teaching them.

This is what is told to a wise son or daughter. Proverbs 13:1 says, "A wise son heeds his father's instruction, But a scoffer does not listen to rebuke." Again, the attitude behind this is very important, and that is why we do not have only the word *obey* but also *honor*. Good sense is developed by listening, hearing, obeying, and honoring.

Again, Ephesians 6:1 says, "Children, obey your parents in the Lord, for this is right." The word *right* comes from the root word *just* or *righteous*. When God says something is right, it is right. Children should be taught to understand that it is

God himself who says this is right. Parents, God says it is right, and God does not have to come and explain why he said it is right. If God said it, then it is so. It is something that cannot be defended because it is right. A child may ask Mom and Dad why obey, and all we can say is the word of God says so, and it is right. You don't need to defend it; it is right. When this word is applied in your life, understanding will come later.

# About the Author

MICHAEL B. ANNANCY IS THE lead and founding pastor of Praise Church, Oklahoma. Michael received his educational degrees from Victory International Bible Training School and Victory International School of Ministry and Missions in Ghana. He did his post-graduate work at Southwestern Christian University in Bethany, Oklahoma, and his graduate work at the University of Oklahoma with a major in counseling.

Pastor Michael has been responsible for promoting the word of God and helping people develop a personal relationship with Jesus. During this time, God has used him to minister and support churches in the United States, Europe, and Africa. Part of his call has been to awaken others to their God-given destiny and in advancing the kingdom of God through equipping leaders.

Prior to his coming to the United States, Michael served as the director of Victory International Bible School of Ministry and Missions in Accra, Ghana, where he played a vital role in shaping the lives of hundreds of ministry students who had dedicated themselves to the calling of God. He also served as a national coordinator and the West and Central Africa coordinator for Operation Christmas Child (Samaritan's Purse)—a gift-filled shoebox program out of Bonne, North Carolina, headed by Franklin Graham (son of Billy Graham). He also served as the pastor in charge of Joshkrisdan Orphanage Home in Ghana, West Africa, founded by John and Libby Moritz, based out of Sheffield, Massachusetts (Hearts of the Father Outreach, Inc.). He also served as an associate pastor of Springs of Live Chapel International and Agape World Outreach International in Accra, Ghana, and International Victory Charismatic Church in Oklahoma.

In August 2010, he felt a stirring in his heart, and God revealed to him that he is being called into a new territory—to open Praise Church, a multicultural and multigenerational family church on a mission to love God, love one another, and exhibit his love in Oklahoma City, Oklahoma.

In April 2015, Pastor Michael stepped out in faith to pursue his course in laying the foundation for a church that will reach Oklahoma City with the love of Jesus Christ. It's with great privilege and honor that he serves as lead pastor of Praise Church and offers a real and powerful experience with Jesus.

Michael and his wife, Wilhemina (Mina), are a dynamic couple with many years of real-life experience in full-time ministry. They met while attending Christ Victory Church in Accra, Ghana, and they are the proud parents of two sons, Derrick and Joel, and a daughter, Michele. They love their children more than words can say. They are active in church and are excited to see what God is going to do through these world changers.